What people are saying about

The Top Ten Mistakes Leaders Make

"Most leadership books have a short shelf life, but Hans' book has endured the test of time. It's a great read on servant leadership."

Rick Warren, pastor, Saddleback Church;
author, *The Purpose Driven Life*

"This is one of the most practical books on leadership I have in my own personal library. If you are serious about becoming a better leader, you will want to read this book."

John C. Maxwell, author, speaker, and founder,
The INJOY Group, Atlanta, Georgia

"Hans' book is a leader's mirror ... you'll see yourself in previously unrevealed ways and learn what it takes to get presentable for effective leadership."

Joseph M. Stowell, author, speaker, and former president,
Moody Bible Institute, Chicago

"Solid concepts. Great quotes. Good stories. Hans Finzel has combined sophisticated leadership theory with practical principles to teach us how to lead. Read this book today and become a better leader tomorrow."

Leith Anderson, pastor, Wooddale Church, Eden Prairie, Minnesota

"I think that chapter 3, 'The Absence of Affirmation,' is worth the price of the book. Leaders today desperately need to learn how to affirm followers and emerging leaders."

Bobby Clinton, professor of leadership, Fuller Theological Seminary School of
Intercultural Studies, Pasadena, California

THE TOP TEN
MISTAKES
LEADERS MAKE

HANS FINZEL

THE TOP TEN
MISTAKES
LEADERS MAKE

HANS FINZEL

David C Cook
transforming lives together

THE TOP TEN MISTAKES LEADERS MAKE
Published by David C. Cook
4050 Lee Vance View
Colorado Springs, CO 80918 U.S.A.

David C. Cook Distribution Canada
55 Woodslee Avenue, Paris, Ontario, Canada N3L 3E5

David C. Cook U.K., Kingsway Communications
Eastbourne, East Sussex BN23 6NT, England

The Web site addresses recommended throughout this book are offered as
a resource to you. These Web sites are not intended in any way to be or imply
an endorsement on the part of David C. Cook, nor do we vouch for their content.

Unless otherwise noted, all Scripture quotations are taken from the *Holy Bible,
New International Version®*. *NIV®*. Copyright © 1973, 1978, 1984 by International
Bible Society. Used by permission of Zondervan. All rights reserved. Scripture quotations marked NASB are taken from the *New American Standard Bible,* © Copyright
1960, 1995 by The Lockman Foundation. Used by permission.

LCCN 2007934655
ISBN 978-0-7814-4549-8
eISBN 978-1-4347-6660-1

© 2007 Hans Finzel

Previously published under the same title by Victor Books® © 1994,
ISBN 1-56476-246-7.

The Team: John Blase, Gudmund Lee, Theresa With, Susan Vannaman
Cover Design: The DesignWorks Group
Cover Photo: Steve Gardner, PixelWorks Studios

Printed in the United States of America
Second Edition 2007

7 8 9 10 11 12 13 14

101910

To our four children,
Mark, Jeremy, Cambria, and Andrew.
It is you—bar none—whom I care most to lead
in the best way possible by the grace of God.

CONTENTS

ACKNOWLEDGMENTS

One of my first big leadership challenges was with my Boy Scout troop as a young Eagle Scout. At fourteen, I was senior patrol leader, the guy who ran all the meetings and decided our troop's direction. It was my first venture into leading others, and I have to admit I enjoyed the power to influence. Through my teen years, I held various jobs, which often transitioned into leadership roles. One that stands out is when I became *head cook,* at age fifteen, on the night shift at a Shoney's Big Boy restaurant in my hometown of Huntsville, Alabama. It seems that from the time I was a teenager I have fallen into roles of leadership—and I have grown to love the challenges. I went on to work through my teens and twenties as a lifeguard, in direct sales, as a truck driver, a carpenter, house painting, and as a senior sales rep with a home security firm.

Through my subsequent two decades of assuming leadership positions, at various jobs in the world of business and in ministry, I had no formal training in the area. All that changed in 1986 when I met Sam Metcalf, president of CRM of Fullerton, California, who has since become one of my mentors (see chapter 7). Sam told me about an unusual professor at the Fuller School of Intercultural Studies in Pasadena, who was pioneering an innovative approach to leadership study for Christian leaders. So I flew to California to meet this unique gentleman and was sold on his approach to leadership training. By September 1987 I was deeply immersed in my doctoral studies under the mentorship of this colorful

individual, Bobby Clinton. Clinton has done more than anyone to revo-
lutionize my view of leadership and to put me on track for what I believe
to be biblical leadership values that will serve me well into the twenty-first
century.

I must also acknowledge the unbelievable support of my wife,
Donna. For more than three decades she has put up with my bursts of
energy that overextend me amid the chaos of an already busy life and
heavy responsibilities. I committed to write the book you hold in your
hands before being selected to the leadership role I now fill in a global
enterprise. This position has consumed most of my attention since I
assumed my role in 1993. I appreciate the many nights and weekends
away from home Donna has allowed to enable me to complete this project, which was so important to me.

My leadership is our leadership. Anything I have learned or done of
value in these years I share in partnership with the great wife God has gra-
ciously given me. And now, fifteen years after I first wrote the original version of this book, the kids have left the nest, but she continues faithfully
at my side in full support of my leadership. I am a blessed man indeed.

INTRODUCTION

The setting was a stuffy, windowless conference room at the local Holiday Inn. Hot, tired, and weary, we were nearing the end of a marathon day of intense scrutiny as my wife, Donna, and I were meeting with our organization's CEO-search committee. I was the primary candidate for becoming the new president, and the committee wanted to ensure no stones were left unturned. This all-day session was the culmination of their six-month investigation into my background. I felt the same emotions people must feel when submitting themselves to the searchlight intensity of Senate confirmation hearings.

One of the gentlemen on my left asked me a question that surprised me: "Hans, tell us why you want to become our new leader."

To put this question in perspective, our organization, WorldVenture, is global. We have a presence in more than sixty countries, with an overseas personnel force of more than 600. In addition, we have a home office in the United States with a staff of more than fifty, and four regional offices throughout North America. The CEO oversees an annual budget of twenty-five million dollars.

"Did I ever *say* I wanted to become the leader?" I answered with a big smile. "You never heard that from my lips!" I went on to explain that I had always been willing during my twelve-year tenure in the organization to accept larger responsibilities. And now I was *willing* to take the top job, "But be very clear that I am willing, not seeking."

I knew that this career move would bring tremendous pressure into my life, my marriage, and my young family. I had a house full with four children, the oldest just reaching his teenage years. Now that I have been in the role for more than a decade, I have bad news for you aspiring leaders out there: It is a lot more intense than I ever imagined! I have now logged twenty-seven years with WorldVenture, including fourteen as president. Leadership is one long journey of constant stress. A woman commented to me one day after I had given a vision talk about our organization, "You must absolutely love your job!" I thought to myself, *Well I suppose … on some days … when the planets are all aligned and everything is actually going right.*

Leadership can be dangerous. To understand this, study world history and the lives of great and terrible leaders and what they accomplished through others. We who are in leadership can, on one hand, move men, women, and mountains for tremendous good. On the other hand, we hold the power to do irreparable damage to our followers by the mistakes we make.

The greater our sphere of leadership influence, the higher our impact on the world around us. And the more people we lead, the greater the potential damage caused through our poor decisions and actions. This is one of the sobering realities we must face when we accept the mantle of leadership.

Good leaders seem to be a scarce commodity today. There are plenty of openings but fewer good candidates. Why is it that so many companies, organizations, churches, and schools are looking for leaders to fill empty slots? Perhaps the problem is not really that new. Thousands of years ago a wise man wrote:

> "I looked for a man among them who would … stand before me in the gap on behalf of the land so I would not have to destroy it, but I found none" (Ezek. 22:30).

Since the first edition of this book was created in the early 1990s, I have had the opportunity to speak with many different leaders from many different walks of life: policemen, teachers, school administrators, corporate leaders, middle management, government agency employees, businessmen, salespeople, family business owners, and, of course, the elders and staff of local churches. I am often asked, "Have you changed your mind about the top ten mistakes fifteen years later?" My answer: Absolutely not! Though I now have a list of the next dozen mistakes leaders make.

My years in the pressure cooker of leadership have confirmed everything I share in this book, and they have encouraged me to add a few new insights that I learned along the way. I have simply tried to share some of the great lessons I've gleaned on leadership that came through my own mistakes. This book is not intended to answer the question of leadership scarcity, but rather to look at what makes a good leader go bad, or better yet, what habits to avoid if you want to help fill the gap and replenish the great leadership famine. It is a resource book for anyone in any kind of leadership role.

If you have read this far, you are no doubt a leader with a leadership challenge. The challenge may be with your own leadership or with someone who leads you. Or it could be with the people you are being asked to lead. I hear from so many readers who work under oppressive leaders. I hope this book is an encouragement to them.

My informal survey of leaders suggests that people fall into leadership more by accident than by design. Through whatever circumstances led them to that point, they are thrown into leadership and become what I call "reluctant leaders." How many actually sign up or apply for leadership positions? It is the kind of role you are chosen for—you usually do not volunteer.

After falling into leadership, we tend to do what comes naturally—we "wing it." And that's what gets leaders into trouble, because good leadership practice is often the opposite of conventional wisdom. It may come naturally, for instance, to treat employees like children, but it is much better to treat them with adult respect—as your most precious resources for success.

Few prepare themselves or volunteer for leadership. It is a calling for the appointed. This seems to be true across the board—in industry, business, and government. And it is equally true if not more so in ministry vocations. Many people who come into positions of leadership in churches or Christian organizations have little or no training in leadership and management. Leaders of Christian enterprises tend to be spiritually qualified but often organizationally illiterate. The problem is, leadership requires both the heart and the head.

The greatest lessons I've learned about good leadership have been through my own mistakes. And from bad examples. Those mistakes and bad examples have helped identify some common patterns in the mistakes leaders tend to make.

So what are the most common pitfalls of leadership? And, can we really learn any good lessons from the bad mistakes of others?

LEARNING GOOD FROM THINGS THAT GO BAD

Years ago my own professional career came to a screeching halt as I fell into a deep, black pit of burnout. The situation stemmed largely from my relationship with the leader above me. I had finished college and graduate school to prepare myself for a successful career in my chosen field. My heart was filled with dreams and visions of how I would make a difference in the world. *Look out world, here I come!* Through my efforts, I began to accomplish a few good things. I was involved with an exciting new venture that was really making a difference.

But my professional track record was about to be derailed, and I never saw it coming. Great leaders challenge people to attempt things they would never try on their own. I met a man who inspired me and challenged me to a great cause. He recruited me with promises of great things to come. I was going to be a part of something much larger than I had ever dreamed of. My wife and I moved to join his team, and the first few years were excellent. Great leaders do that. They inspire us to go places we would never go on our own and to attempt things we never thought we had in us.

Then it happened. At the five-year marker under his leadership, things began to unravel. He lost confidence in me and I in him. Suddenly my world came crashing down around me. Those youthful hopes and early dreams were dashed like waves crashing against ugly, jagged rocks. I lost sight of the future as I fell deep into a valley of depression. My heart, once filled with zeal to do good in a bad world, was suddenly filled with bitterness. I was angry, and that anger arose out of my frustration over broken dreams and unfulfilled promises.

And who was the main cause of my blame? I would be arrogant not to take the blame myself. I was at fault for failing to learn some important lessons in leadership. God was lowering my pride a few hundred notches and teaching me much about my own leadership shortcomings.

Then there was my soon-to-be-former leader. A person with some great qualities but also some equally great shortcomings. I fell from such heights of promise to such depths of despair in part because of his

> GREAT LEADERS INSPIRE US TO GO PLACES WE WOULD NEVER GO ON OUR OWN AND TO ATTEMPT THINGS WE NEVER THOUGHT WE HAD IN US.

actions—and in some respects because of his neglect. This leader, like most, had no clue as to how much power he wielded over his subordinates. Great leaders forget what it feels like to be led. Some have never even experienced "followership," because they have led from the moment they were born—right out of the womb, bossing Mom and Dad around!

Leaders have incredible power for good or ill in people's lives. A few control the destiny of many. But how many of us start out with lofty ideals and dreams, only to be soured by our experiences with other leaders? Before we know it, people lose trust, and the trench warfare begins. Or nothing is said, but confidence in our leadership begins to erode quickly. People resign and walk. Leaders are fired. Division, strife, and backbiting reign. The work, whatever it is, is slowed, damaged, or comes to a screeching halt.

LEADERSHIP IS INFLUENCE

The subject of leadership can be very confusing. If you would ask me to recommend one good book on leadership, I would probably pause and draw a blank. It's not that I don't have shelves of great books on the subject; it's just that they emphasize so many various nuances of the subject. I would ask you what area of leadership you want to read about. One of my top ten favorite general books on the qualities of great leadership is a classic written in 1989: *Leaders,* by Warren Bennis and Burt Nanus. They begin by relating the frustrating history of research into the true nature of great leadership.

Decades of academic analysis have given us more than 350 definitions of leadership. Never have so many labored so long to say so little. Like love, leadership continued to be something everyone knew existed but nobody could define. Many other theories of leadership have come and gone.

Some looked at the leader. Some looked at the situation. None has stood the test of time. With such a track record, it is understandable why leadership research and theory have been so frustrating as to deserve the

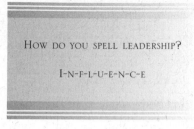

HOW DO YOU SPELL LEADERSHIP?

I-N-F-L-U-E-N-C-E

label "the La Brea Tar Pits" of organizational inquiry. Located in Los Angeles, these asphalt pits house the remains of a long sequence of prehistoric animals that came to investigate but never left the area.

I tend to view the profound process of leadership in terms of a very simple definition: Leadership is *influence*. That's it. A one-word definition. Anyone who *influences* someone else to do something has led that person. Another way to say this might be: *A leader takes people where they would never go on their own.*

DO MOST LEADERS JUST WING IT?

Years have passed since my experience with leadership gone bad. I have forgiven that leader. In fact, to this day I admire him for the many great leadership gifts he has. And I thank him for all he contributed to my life in our years together. He is what I would call a born leader. He inspired me toward greatness. He helped me in countless ways. And hopefully I have learned from his mistakes.

What makes leaders fail? Why are bad leadership habits perpetuated? Because most of us who lead *have neither been formally trained nor had good role models.* So we lead as we were led. We wing it.

At a recent conference of Christian pastors and leaders, the question was raised, "How many of you ever had one course in college or seminary on how to lead effectively?" The results were shocking. Almost no one had

had any formal training. Lacking any training, leaders lead as they were
led. They may be extensively trained in how to do ministry, but not in how
to lead others who minister. Seminaries rarely offer such training.
Churches don't do a very good job of it, either. It is left to books, seminars, tapes, and other informal sources of training to build the leader's
knowledge of skills in leadership.

This problem is not unique to people in ministry. The lack of training and preparation runs the entire spectrum of people in leadership. The
average leader faces at least five problems in learning to lead, each of which
will be addressed with solutions in this book:

1. *Today's leaders replicate the poor leadership habits they have
   observed in others.* We will look at how we imitate what
   we see modeled.

2. *Today's leaders often lack basic skills for common leadership
   demands.* We will look at some positive skills and attitudes that can overcome the top ten mistakes I will
   present.

3. *Today's leaders lack good models and mentoring.* I will illustrate positive leadership values with some real-life examples of good leaders.

4. *Today's leaders lack formal training in leadership.* Since formal training is usually not available for the busy leader,
   this book offers practical insight that he or she can use.

5. *Today's Christian leaders suffer confusion over the conflict
   between secular and biblical leadership values.* This problem is unique for those in ministry. An important
   underpinning of my approach is to highlight the contrast between what the Bible values in leadership (the
   best example of good leadership is Jesus Christ and his

servanthood approach) and what secular leaders often
value (all too often, top-down control).

This book is for those of you who find yourselves called to lead and
are a bit apprehensive about blowing it. And it is for those of you who
struggle under the poor leadership of others. The insights in these pages
apply whether you are leading a company, a ministry, a department, one
or two coworkers, a Girl Scout club, an army platoon, a committee, or
your family.

Today the influence of my generation of leaders, the baby boomers, is
in full swing. But in the not-too-dis-
tant future we will be filling the nurs-
ing homes, and the emerging
generations will be coming into positions of leadership across the land. I
can see a whole new hunger for practical leadership wisdom emerging
among today's young leaders. That
excites me! As the younger generations are being called on to lead everything from Fortune 500 companies

WHY DO NEW LEADERS OFTEN GET A BAD START?

➤ We replicate the poor lead-
  ership habits of others.
➤ We lead as we were led.
➤ We aren't born with leader-
  ship skills.
➤ We lack good models and
  mentors.
➤ We lack formal training.

and family businesses to churches, seminaries, missions, factories, and
even the U.S. government, it is my chance to mentor them as I am able
with lessons I have learned during my years at the wheel.

Top-flight leaders really aren't born; they learn by trial and error. Poor
leadership habits and practices can spawn new generations of poor leaders.
Or they can create enough discomfort that the leader figures out how to
do it right. That has been my own experience, and I offer the notes from
my journey to others who are called to lead.

When my children were young, I enjoyed stealing away from the pressures of my work to take them for bike rides on some of the great riding trails not far from our home. As the dad, it was usually in my hands to determine whether the day would be fun for them, or a disaster. I was the designated leader. If we were to go out for several hours, I would grab the right equipment and supplies for all emergencies. (Actually, to be totally honest, it was their mom who pulled it all together!) We would get tires pumped up, and gather the right clothes, food, and water for the journey. No trip with little ones was complete without being prepared for pitfalls along the way: potholes, sunburn, thirst, windburn, scrapes, bruises, saddle sores, careening cars (therefore, helmets), and fatigue. The best biking equipment in the world is overshadowed by the smallest problem like a tiny leak and no repair kit, or a blazing sun and no sunscreen. I have great memories of those many outings—but they were not without careful preparation.

Leadership is like that. The good you do can be destroyed by the precautions you fail to take. No matter how skilled or gifted we are as leaders, one or two glaring blind spots can ruin our influence. A few bad habits can void the effectiveness of all our talents and accomplishments. The bottom line? An ounce of prevention is worth a pound of good leadership. Thus our need to take a look at some common leadership mistakes.

The privilege of leadership is a high calling ... and an adventure! Perhaps the significance of doing it right is best summed up by George Bernard Shaw in *Man and Superman*:

> This is the true joy in life, the being used for a purpose recognized by yourself as a mighty one; the being a force of nature instead of a feverish selfish little clod of ailments and grievances complaining that the world will not devote itself to making you happy.

I want to be thoroughly used up when I die, for the harder I work the more I live. I rejoice in life for its own sake. Life is no "brief candle" to me. It is a sort of splendid torch which I have got hold of for the moment, and I want to make it burn as brightly as possible before handing it on to future generations. (84)

THE TOP-DOWN ATTITUDE

The Number One Leadership Hang-up

- ➤ The top-down attitude comes naturally to most people.
- ➤ Servant leadership is much more rare.
- ➤ Effective leaders see themselves at the bottom of an inverted pyramid.

I intended to save the best for last, like a David Letterman top-ten countdown. But on second thought, I realize that this top-down attitude problem is like the mother of all leadership hang-ups. If you have it, you will spread it to everything your leadership hands touch. So it must come first as the foundation to everything else I will observe about how not to lead.

At a leadership conference for pastors and their wives in northern California several months ago, I was speaking on the theme of top leadership mistakes. One man came up to me after a session and asked the obvious question: "Which is the top of the top ten?" That was an easy question for me to answer. I believe that the number-one leadership sin is that of *top-down autocratic leadership*.

You would think people would have learned by now, yet it still keeps cropping up: that age-old problem of domineering, autocratic, top-down leadership. Of all the sins of poor leadership, none is greater and none is still committed more often, generation after generation.

> "He that thinketh he leadeth and hath no one following him only taketh a walk."
> —Dr. John Maxwell

The top-down approach to leadership is based on the military model of barking orders to weak underlings. It goes something like this: "I'm in charge here, and the sooner you figure that out the better!" Take, for example, this story related to me by one of my students when I was teaching a course on leadership:

My organization was looking for a new regional leader. Those making the decision had somebody picked out. However, before finalizing it, they were going to meet with different people to receive feedback on the individual they had chosen. I gave them my serious concerns and observations. Even though they took the time to listen to us, they really didn't hear what we were saying. In the end, our input and feedback was rejected. And our predictions came to pass. How did this whole situation make us feel? We concluded that the leaders at the top had already made up their minds regarding their choice, and that, almost as an afterthought, they had decided to talk to us "underlings" to try to get our rubberstamp approval. It made me feel as if they didn't really want or need my input. If they would have listened to us, we would have been spared the pain, misunderstanding, and hurt when it became obvious to everyone that this individual was the wrong choice for leadership.

One blatantly irritating practice of some leaders who exercise a top-down style is the use of knowledge—or really the lack thereof—to keep people in line and in place.

Knowledge in an organization is power. A leader can use this power to dominate underlings by keeping them guessing and in the dark.

Dictators have long recognized that others' knowledge is their worst enemy. I grew up in Alabama in the Deep South, where the whites kept the blacks ignorant so their knowledge could not become dangerous. I'll never forget the day our governor stood before the entrance to the University of Alabama to bar a young black girl from becoming our state's first black student at a white university. It was a sick and mistaken attitude of arrogance that, fortunately for us all, soon crumbled.

WHERE TOP-DOWN SHOWS UP

- ➤ Abusive authority
- ➤ Deplorable delegation
- ➤ Lack of listening
- ➤ Dictatorship in decision making
- ➤ Lack of letting go
- ➤ Egocentric manner

If people are kept in the darkness of ignorance, they are less likely to revolt against a ruthless ruler. For that reason, for years communist border guards were ordered to confiscate current magazines and newspapers from Western tourists. In the years when I traveled in Eastern Europe, the border guards always asked us if we had three categories of "contraband": *weapons, books and magazines, and Bibles.* They knew that if the truth got into the hands of the citizens, the task of maintaining tyranny would become more difficult.

The *Royal Bank Letter*, a Canadian publication, made this observation:

A prophetic expert on the subject of tyranny through ignorance, Adolf
Hitler, wrote in *Mein Kampf* that propaganda, to be effective, must operate on the level of the "most stupid" members of society. Hitler, who
loathed universal education, knew that ignorance goes hand-in-hand
with gullibility. He realized that he could best "work his wicked will," as
Winston Churchill put it, when his audience was kept in the dark.

Top-down leadership can become like a chain reaction. The boss barks
orders to the employee. The employee goes home and barks orders at his
spouse. The spouse barks orders at the children. The children kick the dog,
and the dog chases the neighborhood cat! It comes so naturally to most of
us to be autocratic, but it also happens to be a great leadership mistake.

Why do a lot of people fall into the trap of top-down leadership attitudes? For at least five reasons:

1. *It's traditional.* Historically, autocratic, top-down leadership has been the most commonly practiced method.
   This is true in most of the more than one hundred countries I have visited. Far too many people simply learn this
   method by default.
2. *It's the most common.* Even though much has been written
   about alternative forms of leadership, top-down leadership is still the most common kind.
3. *It's the easiest.* It is much easier to simply tell people what
   to do than to attempt other, much more effective leadership styles.
4. *It comes naturally.* For some reason, the natural self prefers
   to dominate others and to try to amass power that can be

held over other people. Leadership, by nature, seems to
entail one person lording over another.

5. *It reflects the dark side of human nature.* For those of us who
believe what the Bible teaches, humans don't need any help
to be depraved. A naturally sinful nature moves us toward
dominating others and lording over them whenever possible.

CONTRASTING TWO APPROACHES

Much has been said in recent years about new styles of leadership that
oppose the top-down, autocratic style. They come with new labels like
"participatory management," the "flat" organizational style, "democratic
leadership," or the model I prefer, called "servant leadership." Servant leadership embraces all these new models and is built on principles that were laid
out by perhaps the greatest leader this world has ever known—Jesus Christ.

A classic source book on this different kind of leadership is *Servant
Leadership,* written thirty years ago by Robert K. Greenleaf. The book is
subtitled, *A Journey into the Nature of Legitimate Power and Greatness.* He
defines the whole process of servant leadership in these terms:

> A new moral principle is emerging which holds that the only authority
> deserving one's allegiance is that which is freely and knowingly granted
> by the led to the leader in response to, and in proportion to, the clearly
> evident servant stature of the leader. Those who choose to follow this
> principle will not casually accept the authority of existing institutions.
> Rather, they will freely respond only to individuals who are chosen as
> leaders because they are proven and trusted as servants. (9–10)

It is refreshing to me to realize that servant leadership is not new, even
in secular management writings. More than forty years ago a landmark

UNDERSTANDING YOUNG WORKERS

With more and more emerging-generation workers on the scene, managers need to understand what turns them on and off.

TURN-ONS

➤ Recognition and praise
➤ Time spent with managers
➤ Learning how their current work is making them more marketable
➤ Opportunities to learn new things
➤ Fun at work—structured play, harmless practical jokes, cartoons, light competition, and surprises
➤ Small, unexpected rewards for jobs well done

TURN-OFFS

➤ Hearing about the past—especially yours
➤ Inflexibility about time
➤ Workaholism
➤ Being watched and scrutinized
➤ Feeling pressured to convert to traditionalist behavior
➤ Disparaging comments about their generation's tastes and styles
➤ Feeling disrespected

—*Lawrence J. Bradford and Claire Raines,* Twenty-Something

book began the revolution away from dictatorial leadership. In 1960 Douglas McGregor published *The Human Side of Enterprise,* in which he outlined what became known as "Theory X versus Theory Y" leadership style. Basically, McGregor believed that people really did want to do their best work in organizations, and if properly integrated into ownership of the goals of the organization, they would control themselves and do their best.

To fully understand this notion one must look at the book in the context of the times in which it was written. In the 1950s and 1960s, there was a backlash against strong, centralized, authoritarian leadership styles. McGregor rode the wave of that changing attitude in our society and developed his Theory Y leadership model. It was based on respect for individual workers and gave them much more participation in their supervision and direction, with less rigid direction and control in the hands of their supervisors.

McGregor began what I see as a healthy trend toward servant leadership in the business world and helped move organizations toward a healthier model of leadership. His early theories are at the foundation of many popular management philosophies in the 1990s. I have summarized his Theory X versus Theory Y approach in the following chart. As you note the two columns, it is easy to see that Theory X entails the top-down leadership attitude. It never ceases to amaze me that all these years later, the awareness of Theory Y and other leadership alternatives still has not penetrated the mind-set of many world leaders.

Based on a new look at human nature and drawing heavily from motivational theory, Theory Y says that work can be enjoyable, and

THEORY X	THEORY Y
➤ Work is inherently distasteful to most people.	➤ Work is as natural as play, if conditions are favorable.
➤ Most people are not ambitious, have little desire for responsibility, and prefer to be directed.	➤ Self-control is often indispensable in achieving organizational goals.
➤ Most people have little capacity for creativity in solving organizational problems.	➤ The capacity for creativity in solving organizational problems is widely distributed in the population.
➤ Motivation occurs only at the physiological and safety levels.	➤ Motivation occurs at social and self-actualization levels, as well as physiological and security levels.
➤ Most people must be closely controlled and often coerced to achieve organizational goals.	➤ People can be self-directed and creative at work, if properly motivated.
	—Hersey, Blanchard, and Dewey, *Management of Organizational Behavior*

workers can do their best when trusted to motivate themselves in their work. *Workers should be allowed to self-direct and self-control their tasks* out of the respect and trust coming from management.

Theory X focuses on tactics of direction and control through the exercise of authority. Theory Y, on the other hand, focuses on the nature of human relationships—the integration of personal goals with the success of the enterprise.

SUPERIOR OR SERVANT?

What does servant leadership look like in the real world then? Let me give you a couple of examples from my own recent experiences.

Most mornings at the office begin pretty typically for me. I usually have many items on the agenda: read important papers, write important letters, call several important meetings, make numerous important decisions, and answer only the important phone calls. The idea is that I should sit behind my big desk, and others will come to me with their requests.

Wrong! On one particular morning, within an hour of arriving at the office I found myself in the basement, helping clear out shelves and throwing away trash. I was helping my facilities manager prepare a new area for a library that we would build—a directive I had initiated. A servant leader must be willing to get down and dirty with his troops in the implementation of his objectives.

The top-down attitude is defined by people who believe that everyone should serve them, as opposed to believing they should be serving others within the institution. In reality, it seems to me that everyone in our organization rests on my shoulders—I am at the bottom of an inverted pyramid. I spend countless hours helping others be effective by providing them the facts, the energy, the resources, the networks, the information, or whatever else they need to do an effective job. Most of my day is spent laying aside my own priorities to help others fulfill theirs. Sometimes that requires hours of nitty-gritty work alongside others to help them get their jobs done. Recently I spent half an hour searching through a hard disk for a lost file that a secretary desperately needed. Since I knew the most about how to find the files within that computer, I deemed it important to take my time to look for it. (I did find it, by the way, to everyone's great relief!)

My wife Donna works with passion for a company called NSA, based in Memphis, Tennessee. It is a forty-year-old company that deals with the direct sales of nutritional products. Donna has been in love with this employer for years because she is her own boss and the company's mission is to make her successful. She has achieved the top position of National Marketing Director. This company exists for the worker! Unlike so many companies in corporate America that are out to enrich the shareholder and the corporate elite, this company spells out in their mission statement what is most certainly bottom up servant leadership:

THE MISSION OF NSA
"To build a stable and lasting company
that helps as many people as possible
realize their dreams."

Servant leadership is about caring for others more than for ourselves. It is about compassion for everyone who serves the group. It enriches everyone, not just those at the top. Servant leadership requires us to sit and weep with those who weep within our organizations. It requires getting down and dirty when hard work has to be done. There is nothing in my organization that anyone does that I should not be willing to do myself if it promotes the good of us all.

The One Who Showed Us the Way

People follow leaders for many reasons. The chart on page 39 shows "The Five Levels of Leadership" as described by Dr. John Maxwell. He points out clearly that the most effective and authentic type of leadership is that which is based on one's personhood—respect for the leader. People follow you because of who you are and what you represent.

No Desire to Lead

A true and safe leader is likely to be one who has no desire to lead, but is forced into a position of leadership by the inward pressure of the Holy Spirit and the press of the external situation. Such were Moses and David and the Old Testament prophets. I think there was hardly a great leader from Paul to the present day but that was drafted by the Holy Spirit for the task, and commissioned by the Lord of the Church to fill a position he had little heart for. I believe it might be accepted as a fairly reliable rule of thumb that the man who is ambitious to lead is disqualified as a leader. The true leader will have no desire to lord it over God's heritage, but will be humble, gentle, self-sacrificing, and altogether as ready to follow as to lead, when the Spirit makes it clear that a wiser and more gifted man than himself has appeared.

—A. W. Tozer

And so when it comes to servant leadership, there is no better model than Jesus Christ. On the night he was betrayed, Jesus showed his followers just how much he loved them. We read in John 13:1 that he "knew that the time had come for him to leave this world and go to the Father. Having loved his own who were in the world, he now showed them the full extent of his love." At that moment Jesus gave us the ultimate demonstration of servant leadership: he washed his disciples' feet!

The first thing I always notice in this scene is Jesus' all-encompassing power and authority. The foundation for his servanthood was a true realization of his power, position, and prestige. He was God himself in the flesh and had every right to be a dictator. In fact, in my opinion, he is the only man who has ever walked the face of the earth who has had the right to be an absolute autocrat!

Having this foundation, Jesus demonstrated servant leadership by taking off his robe, picking up a towel, and washing his disciples' feet. If I had been there that night, I would have been embarrassed beyond words the moment I saw him kneel before the first disciple. I would have been embarrassed and humiliated, because I had not been willing to lower myself to the same dirty task. Yet Jesus demonstrated that the greatest among his followers would have to become servant to all.

The explanation of Jesus' servant leadership comes at the end of the story, when he says, "I have set you an example that you should do as I have done for you. I tell you the truth, no servant is greater than his master, nor is a messenger greater than the one who sent him. Now that you know these things, you will be blessed if you do them" (vv. 15–17).

Another place in the New Testament that speaks eloquently about servant leadership is 1 Peter 5:1–7:

> To the elders among you, I appeal as a fellow elder, a witness of Christ's sufferings and one who also will share in the glory to be revealed: Be shepherds of God's flock that is under your care, serving as overseers— not because you must, but because you are willing, as God wants you to be; not greedy for money, but eager to serve; *not lording it over those entrusted to you,* but being examples to the flock. And when the Chief Shepherd appears, you will receive the crown of glory that will never fade away.
>
> Young men, in the same way be submissive to those who are older. *All of you, clothe yourselves with humility toward one another,* because,

"God opposes the proud

but gives grace to the humble."

Humble yourselves, therefore, under God's mighty hand, that He may lift you up in due time. Cast all your anxiety on him because he cares for you. (emphasis mine)

FINAL THOUGHTS

What are the alternatives to the top-down attitude hang-up? In terms of leadership style, I would summarize them as:

1. *Participatory management.* Give a group of employees the privilege of input before you move on a course of action. This can be messy and time consuming, but it motivates and inspires people.

2. *Facilitator style.* See your role as that of a facilitator who makes it possible for those who work for you to be successful. You are there to empower others to effective work.

3. *Democratic leadership.* Build a leadership team with a democratic process that enables the group to have a vital role in the nature and direction of the organization.

4. *Flat organizational characteristics.* View yourself as working side by side with others or as leading the charge, but not as being on the top of a giant pyramid. More on this in chapter 5.

5. *Servant leadership.* If Jesus was a servant of his followers, how can I, in my right mind, think that I should be served by those I lead? This is what Jim Collins calls "Level Five Leadership" in his book *Good to Great.* This leader seeks what's best for the organization

over his or her own well-being.

How then can I lead without the arrogance of a top-down attitude? If my desire is to be a servant leader as I maintain my responsibilities of authority in the organization, what are my guiding principles? Try these practices on for size:

➤ Not abusive authority, but servitude (see John 13).

➤ Not deplorable delegation, but freedom for people to be themselves (see Eph. 4).

➤ Not lack of listening, but focus on the needs of others (see Phil. 2).

➤ Not dictatorship, but partners in the process (see 1 Peter 5:1–4).

➤ Not holding on, but letting go with affirmation (1 Thess. 5:11–14).

➤ Not egocentrism, but power for others (Col. 3:12, 13).

> "Christ Jesus … made himself nothing. He made himself nothing, emptied himself—the great kenosis. He made himself no reputation, no image.
>
> "I can recall my father shaking his head and repeating over and over to himself, 'If I only knew what this meant. There is something powerful here. If I only understood it.' Maybe that is why this Scripture has glued itself to my mind and equally disturbs me. Reputation is so important to me. I want to be seen with the right people, remembered in the right light, advertised with my name spelled right, live in the right neighborhood, drive the right kind of car, wear the right kind of clothing. But Jesus made himself of no reputation!"
> —Gayle D. Erwin, *The Jesus Style*

In closing, this ancient legend illustrates perfectly the significance of quiet servant leadership:

As construction began on a magnificent cathedral, an angel came and promised a large reward to the person who made the most important contribution to the finished sanctuary. As the building went up, people speculated about who would win the prize. The architect? The contractor? The woodcutter? The artisans skilled in gold, iron, brass, and glass? Perhaps the carpenter assigned to the detailed grillwork near the altar? Because each workman did his best, the complete church was a masterpiece. But when the moment came to announce the winner of the reward, everyone was surprised. It was given to an old, poorly dressed peasant woman. What had she done? Every day she had faithfully carried hay to the ox that pulled the marble for the stonecutter.

THE FIVE LEVELS OF LEADERSHIP
"Why People Follow Other People"

5. POSITION (Title) "Rights"
   People follow because they have to. Your influence will not extend beyond the lines of your job description. The longer you stay here, the higher the turnover and lower the morale. People begin to limit you, to put fences around you. You can't stay here more than two years.

4. PERMISSION "Relationships"
   People follow because they want to. People will follow you beyond your stated authority. This level allows work to be fun. Caution: Staying too long on this level without rising will cause highly motivated people to become restless.

3. PRODUCTION "Results"
   People follow because of what you have done for the organization. This is where success is sensed by most people. They like you and what you are doing. Problems are fixed with very little effort because of momentum. (Don't let the momentum stop!)

2. PEOPLE DEVELOPMENT "Reproduction"
   People follow because of what you have done for them personally. This is where long-range growth occurs. Your commitment to developing leaders will ensure ongoing growth to the organization and to people. Do whatever you can to achieve and stay on this level.

1. PERSONHOOD "Respect"
   People follow you because of who you are and what you represent. This step is reserved for leaders who have spent years growing people and organizations. Few make it. Those who do are bigger than life!

   —Dr. John Maxwell, *Developing the Leader Within You*

QUICK TIPS FOR LEADERS ON THE GO

THE TOP-DOWN ATTITUDE
The Number One Leadership Hang-up

Big idea: Human nature leads all of us to want to dominate others. The top-down leadership style is all about command and control, and is the opposite of empowerment. When we first move into positions of leadership, we tend to view ourselves on "top" because we have the smarts, personality, and gifting that got us there. The temptation is to dominate followers and oppress them with the habits of command-and-control cultures. The top-down attitude places the leader as the most important person at the top of the organizational pyramid.

➤ *The top-down attitude comes naturally to most people.* It is human nature's default position.

➤ *Servant leadership is much more rare.* This is the person who puts the organization's well-being ahead of his own.

➤ *Effective leaders see themselves at the bottom of an inverted pyramid.* There are many ways to draw organizational charts. The servant leader carries the organization on his or her shoulders as makes it a goal to make everyone else a winner.

The idea of an opposite style leadership that is more servant oriented is not new. For decades some business writers (notably Greenleaf and McGregor) have advocated this approach, but it has only recently gained traction in the halls of mainstream corporate America and the church. Jesus Christ is the greatest example we have of servant leadership in all of history, which he modeled when he laid down his very life for the benefit of his followers.

PUTTING PAPERWORK BEFORE PEOPLEWORK

Confessions of a Type A Personality

➤ The greater the leadership role, the less time there seems to be for people.

➤ The greater the leadership role, the more important "peoplework" is.

➤ People are opportunities, not interruptions.

➤ Only through association is there transformation.

Not long ago the phone companies in Southern California were forced to add yet another area code in Los Angeles. One PR firm offered this explanation: "All the car phones called the answering machines, which dialed into voice mail, then transmitted by modem to beep the PDAs that forwarded the calls via e-mail to fax the message heard 'round L.A.: "Let's do lunch."

All task-oriented type A personalities must learn to slow down and allow people into our lives. It may seem necessary for most of us to pack a full schedule and keep up with e-mails, phone calls, and text messages, but we will only impact people spiritually and permanently by one-on-one contact that can't be substituted. In this age of telecommunications and teleconnecting, there is still no substitute for quiet, prolonged exposure of one soul to another.

I'm of German descent, and therefore tend to be task oriented. Since I find myself in leadership roles, I often think about how my heritage affects my leadership ability. Is it an unfair generalization to say that all Germans are task oriented? Well, think about any German you know. Do they tend to be perfectionists, accomplishers of great deeds, workaholics who rarely relax, and generally rigid in relationships? Probably. Sure, there are exceptions, but not among the many Germans I've known!

My beautiful, relationally oriented wife is always crying out to me, "Hans, stop! Can't you just sit down for an hour and do nothing? Could we just talk?" That is extremely hard for me to do ... to do "nothing." I guess deep down in my task-oriented nature, I see talking as not really accomplishing that much, so I tend toward being an impatient conversationalist—that is, unless I am in a deep discussion that is driving me toward the

SIGNS OF A PAPER PUSHER

- ➤ "People bother me; they are interruptions."
- ➤ "I prefer to be alone ... to get my work done."
- ➤ "This job would be great ... except for the people!"
- ➤ "I'm out of touch with the networks and currents in the workplace."
- ➤ "I'm insensitive; I tend to run over people."
- ➤ "I listen poorly ... if at all."
- ➤ "I'm impatient."
- ➤ "My self-worth is based on accomplishment."

accomplishment of a task. Or unless I am in a situation in which I cannot immediately get to my work and, therefore, have some downtime. When we go camping, I tend to spend my time tinkering with the equipment instead of just relaxing, which I think someone told me was the actual goal of this pastime . Even on Saturdays when I have the day off, I love making a list of projects and chores and checking them off one by one.

I like to use this cultural heritage bent as an illustration to focus on a certain type of behavior. In the area of leadership, it would be called a task-oriented style of leadership. In the psychological realm, it would be termed *obsessive-compulsive*.

WHY DO WE PUT PAPERWORK BEFORE PEOPLE-WORK?

➤ Observed results take priority over unseen relationships.
➤ Task work pushes aside "idle" talk.
➤ The material world dominates the immaterial world.
➤ We feel we are judged by what we do, not by who we are.
➤ Task-oriented type A characteristics.
➤ Relationships don't fit our deadline mentality.

PEOPLE: OPPORTUNITIES OR INTERRUPTIONS?

I have devised a simple test to discover whether a person is task oriented or people oriented. It's unscientific, but completely reliable. When someone walks into your office, or wherever you happen to work, and interrupts your task at hand for the sake of conversation, how do you react? Do you view that person as an interruption or an opportunity? Does your face brighten as your people antenna powers up, or do you grimace inside at this "interruption"? If you relax and converse until the chat has natural closure, you're obviously a people person. But if you press to squirm your way out of the conversation with a bombardment of verbal and nonverbal clues, then you are one of us: the dreaded type As. If a person's gut-level instinct in that situation is to get back to the task at hand at any cost, it is safe to assume that he or she is task oriented.

Nissan Motors used to have an ad slogan that declared, "We Are Driven." Well, task-oriented people are driven. Many leaders I know are so driven that their notebook computers and BlackBerrys are with them constantly, so they don't miss a chance to task in their spare moments. (I love that word as a verb!)

Psychologists and psychiatrists call this type of personality type A. Extreme cases of this type of personality might also be known as "obsessive-compulsive." Type A personality, also known as the type A behavior pattern, is a set of characteristics that includes being impatient, excessively time-conscious, insecure about one's status, highly competitive, hostile and aggressive, and incapable of relaxation. Type A individuals are often highly achieving workaholics who multitask, drive themselves with deadlines, and are unhappy about the smallest of delays. They have been described as stress junkies. For some reason, the ranks of professional Christian workers—especially pastors and leaders—are flooded with these driven people. It is almost necessary to be a workaholic to make it as a

INTERRUPTIONS ARE OUR WORK

"A few years ago I met an old professor at the University of Notre Dame. Looking back on his long life of teaching, he said with a funny twinkle in his eyes: 'I have always been complaining that my work was constantly interrupted, until I slowly discovered that my interruptions were my work.'

"This is the great conversion in life: to recognize and believe that the many unexpected events are not just disturbing interruptions of our projects, but the way in which God molds our hearts and prepares us for his return...."
—Henri J. Nouwen, *Out of Solitude*

Christian leader. Unfortunately, many leaders are poor listeners because of this very problem. And it seems that the cumulative effect of all these type A leaders takes a toll on the character and spirit of the church today. We have all witnessed in the media before the eyes of the world the epidemic of Christian leaders crashing and burning in recent years. Do our organizations require too much of us? Are we all destined for type A burnout? Is there too much demand on our leaders and not enough on relationships?

I have wondered more and more lately if all my own accomplishments are achieving all that much. If you're highly motivated as I am, you love to have hundreds of irons in the fire. And you also might be missing out on the adventure of a lifetime—rediscovering people!

> ## THE MAESTRO AND PEOPLE
>
> "My intention always has been to arrive at human contact without enforcing authority. A musician, after all, is not a military officer. What matters most is human contact. The great mystery of music making *requires real friendship among those who work together*. Every member of the orchestra knows I am with him and her in my heart."
> —Carlo Maria Giulini, former conductor, Los Angeles Philharmonic, as quoted in Bennis and Nanus, *Leaders*

THE TENSION OF PAPERWORK VERSUS PEOPLEWORK

Before I learned better—and I am still learning—my task-oriented leadership style got me into big trouble as a leader and in serious conflict with my coworkers. The organization and the individuals are not the focus here, because the scenario repeated itself constantly in different ways and in many places. Essentially, I ran into conflicts of role expectations, which is one of the greatest sources of conflict between followers and their leaders. The role we see ourselves playing is expressed through our leadership style. It is the "dressing" of our job, how we appear to others. Sometimes the good we are doing in leadership is totally obscured by a style that alienates our followers.

The groups I was responsible to lead had absolutely no criticism on the way I performed my tasks. In fact, they would all agree that I produced perfection to a fault. I never failed in doing my job, but I did fail in the "being" aspect. The problem was that they wanted my attention, and I was always too busy to give it to them. I fulfilled my organizational duties, but neglected those intangible duties of "peoplework"—just being with people and showing that I care. I viewed my role as a leader primarily as taking care of all of the tasks and paperwork of my job. I was trying to serve my followers by taking care of all of their needs logistically. I solved many of their problems and carried the load of the organizational burden, so they could be free to do their work.

But I failed in one great regard—the human element—that subjective, person-to-person contact so essential in ministry. Their conclusion: I didn't care about them. And all this time I thought I was doing them a favor by accomplishing all those tasks for their benefit! It is like the father who works hard all his life to buy his children everything, then wakes up one day to hear them tell him, "You don't care about me." Does he? Of course! Did I care about the people I worked with? Of course! But I lost the opportunity to lead that group, because my style got me into deep trouble. And it got me thinking about my need for a personal leadership style checkup.

TASK-ORIENTED LEADERSHIP

Most successful leaders today tend toward being task oriented. Even if it is not their nature or personality, it seems the job of the modern-day executive leader demands it. We evaluate people by their accomplishments. Task-oriented people are the ones who are put in charge in the first place. They rise to the top of organizations by virtue of the large volume of tasks they have been able to accomplish. Leaders are expected to produce. Steve Jobs, founder of Apple Inc., says that "leaders *ship.*" Leadership guru Ken Blanchard says, "Good thoughts in your head not delivered, mean squat." And the information revolution creates an ever-growing pile of paperwork that the leader must somehow cope with and control. Whatever happened to the notion that the computer would eliminate paper?

> PEOPLE WILL NEVER CARE HOW MUCH YOU KNOW (PAPERWORK) UNTIL THEY KNOW HOW MUCH YOU CARE (PEOPLEWORK).

People tend to be either task oriented or people oriented. The problem is, we have subtly made task orientation more desirable in our leader selection process. But without a healthy emphasis on people, we're actually accomplishing little. Leadership is essentially a people business. Experts confirm that the most effective leaders spend most of their time being with people and solving people problems. The leadership surveys of Warren Bennis and Burt Nanus spell it out in black-and-white: "What we have found is that the higher the rank, the more interpersonal and human the undertaking. Our top executives spend roughly 90 percent of their time concerned with the messiness of people problems" (Bennis and Nanus, *Leaders*).

THE PROBLEM OF MOUNTING PAPERWORK

We live in an age of ever-increasing complexity. Organizations always evolve into more complex bureaucracies rather than into leaner, more streamlined movements. In the information technology explosion, the leader is bombarded with an increasing barrage of paperwork. Computers have added to the proliferation of materials to write and read. Desktop publishing has given everyone a license to publish anything. The Internet has snowballed our need to read. So how can the busy leader cope? Who is to know what to read anymore? How can anyone even see the people through the piles of paper? These problems alone seem to demand a task-oriented leadership style.

Then there is the issue of the type of people attracted to the ministry and selected for leadership in the church world. While I was in graduate school at Dallas Seminary, Dr. Paul Meier of Minirth-Meier Clinics was my professor for Christian Psychology and Personality Development. He told us that psychological testing of all incoming applicants to our school showed that the vast majority of freshmen had type A personalities. In fact, a number of them displayed traits of an obsessive-compulsive personality disorder. Why were they the ones applying? And why were they the ones accepted into the school? Because they managed to complete the best applications with the most accomplishments? Are our graduate school applicants today chosen according to who they are or what they have completed?

And what comes out the other end when the seminarian graduates three or four years later? Are our seminaries producing largely task-oriented leaders? How much training and emphasis do our seminaries place on people skills? When I finished seminary, I felt that I knew how to begin to tackle the tasks of my job. In fact, I was quite confident in the skills I had honed in those four intense years. But soon after arriving at my first work assignment, I was shocked to learn how weak I was in peoplework training. Some pastors love the inside joke, "I love the ministry; it's the people I can't stand!"

In my first demanding leadership experience, I found myself scrambling to learn how to relate to boards, committees, chairpersons, families, counselees—people everywhere! It was frustrating trying to sort out the role of *pastor:* shepherd to the needs of the flock (peoplework) versus administrator of a large organization (production and paperwork). I felt that I had received next to no training in graduate school in the fine art of nitty-gritty peoplework.

Paperwork is increasingly getting out of hand, and many type As in leadership attempt to manage this seemingly unmanageable task in their own ways. Or they ignore the paperwork and are accused of dropping the ball with poor leadership

EXAMPLES OF JESUS' SHEPHERDING TOUCH

- ➤ He knew them (see John 10:14–15).
- ➤ He touched them (see Luke 4:40).
- ➤ He healed them (see Matthew 15:30).
- ➤ He changed them (see Luke 6:40).
- ➤ He mentored them (see John 13:15–17).

skills. Or, more common than not, they crash and burn. Not a lovely sight. Meanwhile, the people in the body of Christ continue to hurt, to cry out for the attention of professionals who have little time to touch their wounds.

WHATEVER HAPPENED TO PEOPLEWORK?

Jesus was a master of peoplework. No doubt about it. So not long ago I decided to read the four gospels and underline all the leadership principles I found that Jesus demonstrated. I made an amazing discovery: *Jesus spent more time touching people and talking to them than doing any other action.* His focus was not on *words,* it was on *compassion.* Jesus was not primarily task oriented, even though he knew he only had a short time to train twelve men to carry on the movement that would change the world.

Touching wounds amid the unbearable pressure to perform tasks— that was the model of Jesus. If you stay alert to the two words *crowd* and *multitude* in the gospels, you will be amazed to see how often the press of crowds smothered him. At the end of one of his busiest days, it is recorded that, "When the sun was setting, the people brought to Jesus all who had various kinds of sickness, and laying his hands on each one, he healed them" (Luke 4:40).

What is leadership all about? People or paper? Obviously, much of our paperwork and production is aimed at helping people. But too often there is little time or energy left for people after the exhausting efforts of accomplishing those tasks. Whether we like to admit it or not, paperwork, deadlines, and crowded calendars often preoccupy us and create a barrier between us and the opportunity for touching people's lives in a transforming way.

INFLUENCING PEOPLE: A TRANSFORMATIONAL ISSUE

As I suggested at the beginning of this book, the heart of leadership is influencing others. For the Christian leader, it is influencing God's people to move toward God's purposes. But isn't one of God's first and greatest purposes the transformation of character? The apostle Paul, greatest accomplisher of tasks in the early church era, had as his driving passion the transformation of peoples' lives: "We proclaim him, admonishing and teaching everyone with all wisdom, *so that we may present everyone perfect in Christ.* To this end I labor, struggling with all his energy, which so powerfully works in me" (Col. 1:28–29, emphasis mine).

That word *perfect* really means "mature" in the original Greek language. We don't make people perfect, but we help move them toward maturity. Every person who aspires to be used by God in his service must have as a prime objective the same passion: to see people's lives changed into Christ's likeness. For the Christian leader, his or her greatest impact will be lives changed through personal influence on followers.

People Change through Direct Contact

I was reminded of the battle to build relationships late one night at Mount Hermon. For six months I had been in my doctoral sabbatical program in Southern California studying with a favorite professor, Bobby Clinton. I had come to his school to "sit at his feet," yet we had not managed to carve out even a half hour to get to know each other personally. Our calendars just didn't mesh. As chance would have it, we both ended up at Mount Hermon in the coastal mountains of northern California for a couple of days, with that rare commodity known as "dead time." We decided to room together and stayed up past midnight one night, taking the time to begin the process of real relationship building.

I learned more of value about Bobby Clinton in three hours that night than in all the dozens of hours of classroom lectures and casual contact on campus.

How are people changed? How is it that we as leaders can influence others to be more mature? The clearest way to answer these questions is to ask one simple question: *As you review your past, what has had the greatest impact on your growth as a leader and as a person?* Has it been books, lectures, or tapes? Sermons or seminars? Classroom experiences? Every survey I have ever heard about regarding this question comes back with one resounding answer: *A person or a number of key people with whom one has had real-life personal contact has been the primary change agent in the person's life.*

It is always direct contact with a person that has the most powerful impact on our lives. Sure we are influenced by many factors in small ways and at a distance, but the most profound changes in our lives come through people whom we have had coffee with, roomed with, gone to a game with, played with, worshipped with, prayed with.

In my office I have created a little "personal hero" wall on the side of one of my bookcases. It is sort of a shrine to my mentors. On this space, I have

WHICH COMES FIRST, THE PERSON OR THE TASK?

"This is a question that has caused tension for centuries. Which is right depends on what you're doing. If you're at a party, it's people first. If you are fighting a fire, it's task first.

"Psalm 78:72 answers the question like a glittering diamond: 'And David shepherded them with integrity of heart; with skillful hands he led them.' The function of a leader is to feed and guide."

—Lorne Sanny, for thirty years, president of the Navigators

been taping up photos of men who have had the greatest impact on my career, people who have profoundly affected my life. It is a growing collection. The older I get, the more I have come to appreciate that I stand on their shoulders in my leadership. Under their photos, I have their name and the years that I connected with them. Every time I look at their faces, they are talking to me ... reminding me to live out what I learned from them. Some of them are no longer living, but their impact on me endures. They made time for me.

The Bible is full of illustrations of the power of influence modeling—people changing people through personal contact. It has been said that Christian growth is caught, not taught. We see this principle throughout the New Testament. Barnabas mentored Paul into a place of powerful usefulness. And Paul mentored Timothy to take over his own life's work. It is obvious that there was a deep personal relationship—not just casual contact at the office or in the classroom—between Paul and Timothy.

Regardless of what orientation one has in leadership style—task or people—effective leaders make room for people. Leaving them out is a big, big mistake.

If you are wired like I am to enjoy working alone and working on tasks, you must reorient yourself to people. People will only be influenced and changed as we allow them into our personal lives.

Make Room for People

Thomas Watson, founder of IBM, built one of the most successful companies in history because he never allowed the organization to replace people as his number-one focus. During one meeting in the early days of IBM, a number of managers were reviewing customer problems with Watson. On the table were eight or ten piles of papers identifying the sources of problems: manufacturing problems, engineering problems, and the like. After much discussion, Watson, a big man, walked slowly to the front of the room and, with a flash of his hand, swept the table clean and sent papers flying all over the room. He said, "There aren't any categories of problems here. There's just one problem: Some of us aren't paying enough attention to our customers." He turned crisply on his heel and walked out, leaving twenty fellows wondering whether or not they still had jobs (Peters and Waterman, *In Search of Excellence*, 159).

It doesn't hurt to take a lesson from a successful company. In the calling of leadership, people must take priority over paper and production. Yes, we may tend toward one style because of our personalities. But we cannot use that as an excuse to ignore and avoid people.

Final Thoughts

Bill Clinton won the election in November 1992 largely because people in America wanted change and because his handlers helped him focus. He focused on what people cared about most. In their war room, the governor's key aides put up a huge banner to remind them daily of their target: "It's the economy, stupid." I have to remind myself constantly that as a leader my banner must read, "IT'S THE PEOPLE, STUPID." If I neglect this advice, I am indeed the stupid one.

Someone has said that a man's best friend, aside from the dog, is the wastebasket. How often do I find myself lost in the paperwork and production work of ministry and forget to stay connected to the people? My predecessor at WorldVenture, Dr. Warren Webster, had a slogan on his desk that he lived out: "People Count." He was right, and he left me a hard act to follow.

We task-oriented compulsives are fanatics about the future. We live there. I am always planning and working for goals out there in the distance. My preoccupation is chasing that shooting star, that next great task I want to accomplish. It is hard for me to sit still in the here and now, because I have so many irons in the fire for the greater day "out there." It is as if a giant magnet is always pulling my attention and energy into the future.

But every once in a while I stop and take time to look back. I ask myself, *OK, Hans, if it were all over today, what do you have to show for yourself?* If I had no more time left to heap up more accomplishments, would I be satisfied with what my life turned out to be? My answer is quite sobering: The things I look back on and feel a lasting sense of accomplishment about always have to do with the people I have influenced— people who are different, in a positive way, because their lives intersected with mine at some

HOW TO PUSH THE PAPER ASIDE

- Love your wastebasket.
- Do lunches away from work.
- Take time off with your coworkers, spouse, children, and friends.
- Plan getaways with combinations of the above.
- Pray for people.
- Exercise with your colleagues.
- Change locations to get out among people.
- Delegate more.
- Learn to "ransack" instead of reading everything.
- See people as priority one.
- MbWA—Manage by Wandering Around.

point. In rare moments of my life, with not enough frequency, I have allowed others to come into my life and have laid aside my agenda for theirs.

When someone comes into my office or interrupts me on the phone, my gut reaction is to see it as an interruption. But during the past decade I have finally been changing. I am learning to make room for people in my life. When all is said and done, the crowns of my achievements will not be the systems I managed, the things I wrote, or the buildings I built, but the people I personally, permanently influenced through direct contact. Who knows, maybe someday I will be up on someone else's hero wall.

THREADS

Sometimes you just connect,
like that,
no big thing maybe but something beyond the
    usual business stuff.
It comes and goes quickly
so you have to pay attention,
a change in the eyes
when you ask about the family,
a pain flickering behind the statistics
about a boy and a girl in school,
or about seeing them every other Sunday.
An older guy talks about his bride,
a little affectation after twenty-five years.
A hot-eyed achiever laughs before you want him
    to.
Someone tells about his wife's job
or why she quit working to stay home.
An old joker needs another laugh on the way to
    retirement.
A woman says she spends a lot of her salary on
    an au pair
and a good one is hard to find
but worth it because there's nothing more
    important
than the baby.
Listen.
In every office
you hear the threads
of love and joy and fear and guilt,
the cries for celebration and reassurance,
and somehow you know that connecting those
    threads is what you are supposed to do,
and business takes care of itself.
—James A. Autry, *Love and Profit*

QUICK TIPS FOR LEADERS ON THE GO

PUTTING PAPERWORK BEFORE PEOPLEWORK
Confessions of a Type A Personality

Big Idea: Successful leaders have to master great people skills. The higher one rises in his or her leadership role, the more his or her job will become about working with people and spending critical time with them. Yet paperwork threatens that success as we are buried in distractions that keep us away from tending those we need to. Leaders have to learn to manage the paper flow to stay in touch with their people.

> ➤ *The greater the leadership role, the less time there seems to be for people*—leaders have to be readers, but that itself creates a huge problem of paper overload. Computers have not reduced paperwork, in fact they have increased it! Computers and the internet have exponentially increased distractions for busy leaders.

> ➤ *The greater the leadership role, the more important peoplework is*—successful leaders know how to work with people, and it is those people skills that keep them effective. The higher we travel in leadership responsibility, the more our success hinges on spending time with our key staff members in the art of peoplework.

➤ *People are opportunities, not interruptions*—many successful leaders have type A personalities and are driven to accomplish tasks. We have to lay aside tasks at times and see people as our real work.

➤ *Only through association is there transformation*—we cannot change people if we do not spend time with them. People who do not change their minds can't change anything, and it takes face time with people to see such transformation.

THE ABSENCE
OF
AFFIRMATION

*What Could Be Better
Than a Pay Raise?*

➤ Everyone thrives on affirmation and praise.

➤ We wildly underestimate the power of the tiniest personal touch of kindness.

➤ Learn to read the varying levels of affirmation your people need.

After thirty years of marriage, his wife was finally ready to throw in the towel. "I have had it, living with you," she moaned in disgust. "You never tell me you love me. It has been years since I have heard those three words come out of your mouth." In a stoic, cool manner the husband replied, "Look, I told you I loved you when we got married—if I change my mind I'll let you know."

Organizational researchers have been telling us for years that affirmation motivates people much more than financial incentives, but we still don't get it. People thrive on praise. It does more to keep people fulfilled than fortune or fame could do.

How many bosses expect their associates to run on autopilot, as did the hardhearted husband? Do you work for someone who expects the impossible but never encourages you? If you do, I know you are having a hard time at your job. Do you have people who work for you, whom you never encourage with a kind word of appreciation or a note of encouragement? Let them know you appreciate them, and watch their reactions!

I have a great assistant who has been working for me for twelve years. Joyce is a true professional who makes me look good every day. I often jot her words of appreciation on little sticky notes. Once not long ago I discovered to my surprise that she keeps all those notes. She cherishes affirmation, as does everyone. There is little resemblance between the people we work with and the Energizer Bunny. That pink bunny keeps showing up and going and going and going. Humans couldn't be more opposite. They need to have their emotional batteries charged often. I have seen— even in some quarters of my own organization—an attitude that people are expected to work out of a sense of duty, so why bother with this thing called praise? Christian organizations are sometimes the worst, because there is the attitude that "they are working for God, and he will reward them for their labors." Some even argue that it builds egos to give men praise, therefore, it is unspiritual and is to be avoided at all costs. I find that a pretty sad argument against lavishing your coworkers with affirmation and recognition for a job well done. Yes, I am working for that final pat on the back in the sky, "Well done, good and faithful servant." But I think God expects me to pat others on the back along the way.

I am reminded of an example of this principle from my own family that happened when my children were still very young. For months my five-year-old had wanted Rollerblades like his two older brothers, but we just didn't want to endanger our "baby." After running out of excuses to delay the purchase, we finally gave in and picked out a nice pair that should have lasted him for a good year or so. After the purchase, the six of us stopped off for a quick supper, during which Andrew could, of course, think of nothing but those blades. Though it was dark, we promised him that he could take them for a spin as soon as we got home.

When we got home and Andrew tried them on for the first time, he looked about as balanced as a brand new pony trying to take its first steps. Wobbly and unsure of himself, he insisted (to my delight) on hanging on to me as I pulled him up and down the driveway. In fact, my twelve-year-old, Mark, got into the act as Andrew hung between us, dragging his feet as they kept rolling out from under him.

But just two days later, do you think Andrew was still hanging on to us for support? Not a chance. As a matter of fact, in no time, he was out playing goalie in a street hockey game with the neighborhood crew. Andrew needed a great amount of support in the early stages of this new learning experience, but he soon developed his own "skate legs."

> ## COMPLIMENTS ARE SOLUBLE
>
> "One of the commodities in life that most people can't get enough of is compliments. The ego is never so intact that one can't find a hole in which to plug a little praise. But, compliments by their very nature are highly biodegradable and tend to dissolve hours or days after we receive them—which is why we can always use another."
> —Phyllis Theroux

Affirming those who work for and with us follows the same principle. They need the most encouragement at the early stages of a new job or assignment. Which reminds me of another story—an experience my neighbor Keith once had upon changing careers. After much fear and second-guessing, Keith quit his job as a salesman of heating and air-conditioning products to begin a new career in the home mortgage business. "So how is it going, Keith?" I asked as we settled down in our booth for a quiet evening of conversation. "I feel worthless," was his reaction. "Everything is new to me, and I don't seem to get anything right the first time around."

I told Keith that it reminded me of the trauma we went through when we moved to a foreign country awhile back—we felt like helpless children starting life from scratch. It seemed to Keith that there was nothing about this job that related to any of his past experiences. In his former job, he was a top salesman with a great sense of personal pride in his abilities. Now he was back to square one.

I'll never forget what Keith said next: "I lap up every little word of encouragement like a thirsty puppy. It's the only thing that keeps me going." Oftentimes, we have no idea how much those little pats on the back mean to those around us.

Different Strokes

Remember, though, that the people who work with you will require different amounts and different kinds of affirmation. In fact, I have come to see the varying needs for affirmation as a sort of continuum, as shown in the chart on the next page. Most people fall somewhere in the middle of this chart, though I find more people tend toward being desperados—people who often find themselves alone and are desperate for affirmation—than self-reliant islands who just wish to be left alone. Here's how I would describe the various types of affirmation needs on this continuum:

Desperados. This is the group who can't get enough praise and good strokes. They are desperate for approbation. "Warm-Fuzzy" is their middle name. One person who works for me always seems to be on the brink of resigning, until we pull him back with lavish praise and affirmation. Most new workers in a group need this kind of attention to assure them that they are going to be welcomed and are doing a good job. In the early stage of his new job, Keith was definitely a desperado.

THE AFFIRMATION CONTINUUM

Desperados	Autopilots
➤ Little confidence	➤ Self-reliant
➤ Lap up affirmation	➤ Skeptical of affirmation
➤ "The more the better"	➤ "Leave me alone"
➤ Fragile	➤ Tough as nails

Up-and-downers. For a long time, Mary will go along just fine with little need of attention. But then she will enter into an emotional valley. Personal problems? Trouble at home with the children? Who knows, but she will begin to show signs of needing more attention. A good leader learns to read these signs in the countenance of his people. Another one of my employees follows this pattern. If I have not interacted with him for many long weeks, I then begin to get nervous that he may be down. So I seek him out and assure him that he is still just as valuable as he was the last time I pumped him up. Recently, he was sick for a few days and missed work. I slipped a card under his door, so he would find it first thing upon arriving back in the office. In it I simply told him that he was missed. He is single, and I think that makes it even more important, since he was home alone. I told him, "We missed your being around, not for what you do but for who you are as part of us." It meant a lot to him.

"Normal" people. Are there any? If so, I assure you they're a dying

breed! Some people who come from stable homes may not need as much affirmation as others, but we are seeing more and more people coming from unstable backgrounds. The more unstable the background, the more they are going to need your regular affirmation. My observation is that the younger generation needs more nurturing than the more rugged veterans of the corporate world.

Autopilots. These are the Energizer bunnies. I have known a few people through the years who really didn't need any encouragement. They were so strong and so busy that any attempts at praising them would seem like nothing more than a pesky annoyance. They would brush it off with a look of confusion. There are also a few people who view attempts at praise with great suspicion. *What does he want from me? What is coming next? Is he buttering me up for the kill?* These are skeptics and people who have probably had bad experiences with others taking advantage of them. With them, all we need to do is cultivate kindness.

THANK-YOU NOTES: A TINY HUMAN TOUCH GOES A LONG WAY

"We wildly underestimate the power of the tiniest personal touch. And of all personal touches, I find the short, hand-written 'nice job' note to have the highest impact. (It even seems to beat a call—something about the tangibility.)

"A former boss (who's gone on to a highly successful career) religiously took about 15 minutes (max) at the end of each day, at 5:30 p.m., 6:30 p.m., whenever, to jot a half-dozen paragraph-long notes to people who'd given him time during the day or who'd made a provocative remark at some meeting. I remember him saying that he was dumbfounded by the number of recipients who subsequently thanked him for thanking them."

—Tom Peters, "Management Excellence," *The Business Journal*

This concept of different strokes for different folks is not really new. In the New Testament Paul says, "And we urge you, brothers, warn those who are idle, encourage the timid, help the weak, be patient with everyone" (1 Thess. 5:14).

This whole business of affirming those who work with and for us is very simple: Do it! Keep boxes of various kinds of note cards and encouragement cards at your desk at the ready. Oftentimes you need not even bother with a separate card or letter when sending an affirmation. Just scribble a "good job, well done " on the margin of a memo, or shoot a quick e-mail reply. This communicates two things: First, that you actually read this piece of information, which is a miracle in itself because of the paper factory most of us work in these days! And second, this conveys to your employee that you thought he or she did a good job. Those who work with me have learned that I don't automatically praise everything, for I have high standards and ideals. But there is always something good to be found, even in the people most difficult to work with. I might have to give someone a shot in the arm from time to time, but I don't always have to let them feel the needle.

Paul finishes with this thought: "Make sure that nobody pays back wrong for wrong [there's enough of that going around!], but always try to be kind to each other and to everyone else" (v. 15). I take this to heart in leadership. Every day I have as a goal of writing at least three words of kindness to someone. I once read a poem that led me to develop the practice of not putting off praise if I think it is deserved:

> If you know that praise is due him
> Now's the time to give it,
> For he cannot read his tombstone when he's dead.

FINAL THOUGHTS

Back when our twins were little, they often demonstrated another great lesson about affirming good work done by others: Affirmation doesn't last. It needs to be replenished after long dry periods. I have always traveled a lot in my work, so I would often go through the unpleasant and downright gut-wrenching task of saying good-bye to all my kids before a trip. The good news is that they loved me and enjoyed lots of hugs and kisses before my departure to the airport. The twins and I had this thing about "filling my cup" before I left home. If my trip lasted five days, I would tell them as I said good-bye, "Now I need my cup filled up with five days of hugs and kisses." They pounced on me as we rolled on the floor in a delightful sea of love, hugs, and kisses. They filled my cup. And in a different but similar way, I have to fill the cups of my coworkers as they run dry in the heat of their work.

Bottom line? Here are some verses from the New Testament that go with each of these encouragements.

Listening. "Listen" is the most important word in a leader's language. Just because we are the leaders does not mean we are the only ones with a voice. The L in leader stands for listening (see James 1:19).

Empathizing. If others are happy, share their joy. If there is deep tragedy in their lives, stop everything and weep with them (see Rom. 12:15).

Comforting. We have gone through so much ourselves, and those experiences give us the richness as leaders to be able to comfort others when they go through the same pain (see 2 Cor. 1:3–4).

Carrying burdens. This, after all, is the way we "fulfill the law of Christ" (Gal. 6:2).

Encouraging. Let people know often they are doing a good job. Look for the good and point it out, and you'll see more and more good come from your colleagues. "Therefore encourage one another and build each other up, just as in fact you are doing" (1 Thess. 5:11).

APPRECIATE THE EXTRA EFFORT

Former IBM vice president Buck Rodgers recalls the advice of a newspaper columnist, Dr. George Crane, which he read as a teenager. Crane proposed the "Three-Compliments-a-Day Club." He believed that if you "joined" this club, each day you would:

➤ be motivated to look for good around you,
➤ make at least three people happy,
➤ feel good about yourself, and
➤ people would be drawn to you.

Rodgers says the idea seems pretty corny now, but it works. He suggests these embellishments:

1. *Get out of your office.* When someone does a good job, pay him or her a visit to say thanks. It'll make a bigger impact than a memo, a phone call, or an invitation to your office.

2. *Don't let good work be secret.* Ask managers under you to inform you of their subordinates' accomplishments. Employees are discouraged when their special efforts go unnoticed. They may feel it was wasted effort or, worse, think their boss is taking credit for their work. Rodgers always sends them a handwritten note of appreciation.

3. *Thank people publicly.* Formalize thanks whenever possible, in house organs, memos, at meetings, and at conferences.

—Buck Rodgers, *Getting the Best out of Yourself and Others*

QUICK TIPS FOR LEADERS ON THE GO

THE ABSENCE OF AFFIRMATION
What Could Be Better Than a Pay Raise?

Big Idea: Poor leaders demand a great deal from people and never give them a pat on the back for a job well done. Effective leaders realize that most people are motivated more by affirmation and encouragement rather than by financial reward. A huge leadership mistake is to neglect this emotional support that our followers so desperately need. It is the source of high turnover in many organizations and companies, as people leave to find more empowering leadership cultures.

> ➤ *Everyone thrives on affirmation and praise*—since the time we were children we have all loved to get praise for a job well done. Our need for affirmation does not diminish as we grow older!

> ➤ *We wildly underestimate the power of the tiniest personal touch of kindness*—for many people, words of affirmation are at the top of their love languages. Encouraging words give people the fuel to go on even in the most intense work environments. Show love to your workers and they will follow you anywhere!

> ➤ *Learn to read the varying levels of affirmation your people need*—different people who work for you need different degrees and amounts of affirmation. Learn how to read your followers and dish out the encouragement accordingly.

Leaders have to show their followers that they care. If you are the kind of leader that lets people know how they are doing, they will follow you anywhere. It is all about affirmation of good work performed for the common good. We celebrate excellent accomplishments. Yes, the word "love" is not out of bounds in the workplace, as the old adage goes: *People will never care how much you know until they know how much you care.*

4

No Room for Mavericks

They Bring Us the Future!

➤ Mavericks can save us from the slide toward institutionalism.

➤ Large organizations usually kill off mavericks before they can take root.

➤ Mavericks make messes by their very nature—the good messes institutions need.

➤ Learn to recognize truly useful mavericks.

Bill and Mary sat on the couch in my office and spilled their wounded emotions for more than an hour. Here were two extremely gifted individuals who had helped grow their local church very aggressively through their entrepreneurial zeal. Of the entire team of five families, of which they were a part, Bill and Mary had the greatest giftedness in the areas of growing, expanding, and building. Yet they are mavericks, and after just two years their team rejected them for not "playing by the rules." They became outcasts. The word that was relayed to me from the team was, "Don't send them back. We don't want them."

And what are those rules that Bill and Mary broke? As I pried for their offense, all I found was a lack of boring institutional conformity. Like many others who live on the radical fringes of organizations, Bill and Mary have a hard time fitting into a rigid bureaucracy. They are mavericks and need freedom to fly.

> "I'm looking for a lot of men with an infinite capacity for not knowing what can't be done."
> —Henry Ford

Recently I led my senior staff through a discussion at one of our planning retreats on the topic of making room for creative people. I challenged them with this question: "Have we made it impossible for bright rising stars and maverick go-getters to live within our organization?" When we become too preoccupied with policy, procedure, and the fine-tuning of conformity to organizational standards, in effect, we squeeze out some of our most gifted people.

Organizations have this nasty habit of becoming institutions. And institutions have this great tendency to fade into irrelevance. Movements become monuments. Inspiration becomes nostalgic. The tragedy of this often-repeated story is that the older an organization gets, the less room there is for the entrepreneurially gifted. Mavericks are messy by nature, and calcified organizations chew them up and spit them out with their rigidity. Mavericks are necessary for us to be creative. The dictionary defines maverick as "an independent individual who does not go along with a group or party." The word comes from the 1870s when a famous pioneer in the wild western United States refused to brand his cattle. His name was Samuel A. Maverick. Mavericks are free spirits that have always been misunderstood.

This is as true in the church as it is in the business world. Organizations follow a pattern as they move from passion to paralysis, from the apostolic to the mechanistic! This pattern seems to follow the very pattern of the human life cycle, from birth to adolescence to the most productive adult years, and eventually to death. Even organizations that don't die often look and act dead.

When I became president and CEO of WorldVenture fifteen years ago, the company was celebrating its fiftieth anniversary. There were a lot of very proud moments in that history, but to me—any fifty-year-old is going to have issues! It has been my obsession these years to reinvent the organization from inside out and from top to bottom. There is very little I have left unchanged, because the world today is so different than the world that existed when we were founded in 1943. We were in a death spiral in our life cycle and I was determined to turn it around.

Let me illustrate this cycle of life with the following chart. The time when mavericks are most crucial is during the entrepreneur years of expansion in childhood and adolescence and right after the crest during the graying years, when organizations need to be "born again." One reason the

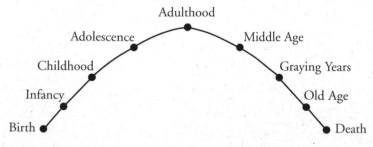

THE LIFE CYCLE OF ORGANIZATIONS

story of Bill and Mary crushed me so deeply was that their church really needed their help but didn't know it. The organization was dying and needed them desperately at that stage in its life cycle. But I am amazed at how many people live in denial during these days of sad decline. They reject the very people that can bring them new life.

Birth. One or two individuals or families decide to try something new. They start a new business, plant a new church, or embark on some new enterprise that will create the new life of an organization.

Infancy. The fragile new organization needs loads of tender loving care and constant feeding and pampering in these trying days of survival. And as new parents discover, there are many costs and few paybacks beyond the joy of seeing the new life you have created.

Childhood. The early, unsure days of floundering youth. First steps are taken amid the bruises and bumps that come with childhood. Great strides in learning are taking place.

Adolescence. The identity crisis comes once the organization is up and running, usually between five and ten years out, when the original founding principles are questioned by the growing number of new members who were not there at the beginning. Great growth pains happen during this rite of passage to adulthood.

Adulthood. The organization is now in its prime, fully staffed, and functioning the way it was intended to from the beginning. These are great productive years, as things are going right and goals are being accomplished in grand style.

Middle age. As in human midlife, things begin to slow down, and some of the zest and zeal of the peak years starts to wane. Settling for limited objectives is a large part of the pattern here.

Graying years. In these years, institutionalization, or even fossilization, is taking place. The preservation of the organization becomes the chief end, and new ideas are discouraged because they upset the established routines of the decades. "We've always done it that way" is the theme song of the graying years.

Old age. If the organization is still around, it is probably maintaining a bare existence with a tiny market share of whatever it does. Nothing is happening, no one notices it, and things are quiet in the orderly hallways and boardrooms. Many churches in our land are in this condition, and can go on for years with the reserves of a few generous estates.

Death. I wish more organizations would take this bold step and declare themselves finished when they have fulfilled their usefulness. Every organization sooner or later must cease to have life—at least life as they once understood it—and we should allow each generation the privilege of creating its own vehicles to accomplish its ideals.

Birth, life, aging, and death: the natural order of creation. What do these life cycles have to do with mavericks? It should be obvious by now that the older an organization, the less room for truly creative people. In the early years of a growing new organization, entrepreneurial vision and zeal is the very lifeblood that gets the group going. Whether a local church is trying to attract new members or a business is going after a new market share, it takes creative vision and go-getters to get things moving.

One of my students asked me the obvious question about the life-cycle chart: "Can the decline down the other side of the curve be avoided, or is it inevitable?" I have grown more skeptical as years have gone by. I have viewed the comings and goings of organizations, which I call the ebb and flow of organizational life. There can be a rebirth, but it takes a strong dose of new blood—young, maverick blood—to arrest the slide down the far side of the life-cycle curve.

Most people who get to know me find that under the reserved German facade is a zealous maverick. So why would a fifty-year-old

THE TEN COMMANDMENTS OF ORGANIZATIONAL PARALYSIS

How to Put Mavericks in Their Place:

1. "That's impossible."
2. "We don't do it that way."
3. "We tried something like that before and it didn't work."
4. "I wish it were that easy."
5. "It's against policy to do it that way."
6. "When you've been around a little longer, you'll understand."
7. "Who gave you permission to change the rules?"
8. "How dare you suggest that what we are doing is wrong!"
9. "If you had been in this field as long as I have, you would understand that what you are suggesting is absolutely absurd!"
10. "That's too radical a change for us."

organization hire a forty-year-old zealot like me to run things? I applaud the board of directors of our organization, not for selecting me, but for taking a gamble on putting a maverick in charge. We needed it at that time of our life cycle. We had been in middle age, and many of the warning signs of the approaching graying years of institutional life were appearing in our midst. When the board of directors was interviewing me, they asked me for my greatest fear for our organization, my gravest concern as we looked into the future. That was an easy question to answer for an organization like ours: "My greatest fear is that our best days are behind us. I loathe the thought that we should fade into irrelevance."

One of the men who had a profound role of mentorship in my life in the 1980s was a fine gentleman by the name of Arno Enns. He has a prominent place on my hero wall. Most people won't recognize his name, but the top ranks of our organization today are filled with men and women he mentored.

For ten years Arno was my boss and immediate supervisor. But he was more than that. After my own father died in 1984, he became like another dad for me. Now Arno is by his very nature cautious and process oriented: Risk taking is not natural for him. But he believed in me, and though I was a maverick in the organization, he cultivated me and harnessed that zeal. He gave me the opportunity to open doors in Eastern Europe in the early 1980s.

An incident in 1982 stands out as an example of how Arno was flexible enough to make room for me. We were living in Vienna, Austria, and making forays into Eastern Europe as part of an underground leadership development network. In the early months of 1982 I relayed a request back to him that I wanted to spend $3,900 for a personal computer. Remember, that was 1982. Most people had never heard of Steve Jobs, and the IBM PC had yet to be released. I was going to purchase a Tandy Radio Shack TRS Model III personal computer to use for writing and database chores. I was, perhaps, the first person in our overseas organization to make such a request. "Why would anyone need a personal computer?" was the general notion back then.

But Arno was different. He believed in me and thought that perhaps this was the way of the future. He listened to my arguments and authorized the purchase as a sound one. It is partly because of that kind of visionary thinking that I have stuck with Arno and our organization all these years. And now, at the helm myself, I have a passion to make room for the next generation of mavericks. Arno is now in his eighties and long retired, but he still sends me articles to read that refresh my spirit and challenge me to lead outside the box! He is a living reminder that you can be eighty years old (that's eighty years young to you, Arno!) and still be a maverick!

MAKE ROOM FOR MAVERICKS

Webster's Dictionary defines a maverick as, "a pioneer, an independent individual who does not go along with a group." Synonyms for

SOME MAVERICKS WHO MADE A DIFFERENCE

➤ *The apostle Paul.* What a turn-
around! He went from being
an outside destroyer to an
inside promoter.
➤ *Martin Luther.* He nailed his
convictions on a door, so the
establishment couldn't miss it.
➤ *William Carey.* When his
superiors told him to sit down
and shut up, he ignored them
and became a mission hero
and father of the modern mis-
sionary movement.
➤ *Lee Iacocca.* He came from
outside to reinvent Chrysler
from the top down.
➤ *Chuck Colson.* From Nixon
hatchet man, then a prison
cell, he's now a modern-day
prophetic voice for evangelical
Christians.
➤ *Martin Luther King Jr.* He had
a dream he was willing to die
for, and he changed the very
fabric of American life.
➤ *Steve Jobs.* Beginning in his
garage with nothing but radical new ideas, he brought IBM
to its knees. Then years later
he did it again—reinventing
the music industry.

maverick include "nonconformist,"
"heretic," "dissident," "dissenter,"
and "separatist." If you think
about it, Jesus was a maverick and
was eventually destroyed by the
institutional religious body he
came to redeem. And you thought
you had it tough getting your ideas
through!

One reason I love reading the
Bible is that it is filled with the stories of men and women who were
nonconformists, who didn't meet
the norms of society. I relate to
them! The Bible is filled with mavericks and revolutionaries that
changed the world. *Moses* was an
outsider whom God chose to bring
renewal to his people. *Joseph* was left
for dead by his brothers. *Peter* was a
maverick from the start, but Jesus
never cast him aside for his raw
edge, instead he cultivated it and
harnessed it. Then, of course, there
was that great Pharisee of Pharisees,
Paul, who, like Martin Luther,
began in the bosom of the institution but was soon coloring outside
the lines. Isn't it just like God to

make one of the chief supporters of the "old" into one of the strongest advocates for the "new"?

A few years ago I read a fascinating book that traces the expansion of Christianity from the perspective of those who made it happen, *From Jerusalem to Irian Jaya,* by Ruth Tucker. It records the simple truth that the greatest strides in the advancement of Christianity have come from the radical fringe, not the institutional core of the church. Likewise, strange inventors such as Thomas Edison and George Washington Carver have brought the business and industrial worlds from one major era to another. Chester Carlson, who invented the Xerox process, was laughed out of town before he finally patented his idea. The 3M company encourages mavericks; the man who invented Post-it notes did it on company time even though it was a personal project. A Swiss watchmaker invented the quartz watch. Unfortunately, his superiors rejected the idea, so the Japanese and Americans patented it, and Switzerland went from an 85 percent global market share of watches to less than 15 percent.

I fear what mavericks are going to do next in my own organization—but not as much as what I fear will happen if we lose them and they end up doing it for someone else!

BREATHING ROOM AND FLEXIBILITY

One of the best ways to take the wind out of the sails of visionaries is to send their ideas to a committee. Here are some comments about committees:

➤ An elephant is a horse designed by a committee.

➤ A committee keeps minutes and wastes hours.

➤ The best committee has three members—if two of them are out of town.

"The photograph is of no commercial value."
—Thomas Edison, remarking on his own invention in 1880

"There is no likelihood man can ever tap the power of the atom."
—Robert Millikan, Nobel Prize winner in physics, 1920

"It is an idle dream to imagine that automobiles will take the place of railways in the long-distance movement of passengers."
—American Road Congress, 1913

"I think there is a world market for maybe five computers."
—Thomas J. Watson Sr., chairman of IBM, 1943

"There is no reason for any individual to have a computer in their home."
—Ken Olsen, president of Digital Equipment Corporation, 1977

—Joel Barker, *Future Edge*

➤ A committee is made up of the unfit trying to lead the unwilling to do the unnecessary.

➤ A committee is a collection of individuals who separately do nothing and together decide that nothing can be done.

It is a big mistake to stifle your brightest stars with the harnesses of endless committees, procedures, and paperwork. As I mentioned in chapter 1 on the top-down attitude, our understanding of leadership has been going through a paradigm revolution these past couple of decades. The old way, exemplified by Henry Ford's production line, called for top managers to analyze the work that needed to be done, then devise detailed rules anyone could follow. Managers, divorced from the actual work, became bureaucrats while their frustrated subordinates tightened the bolts.

Those methods worked well during most of the past century, but they won't help us much in this one. But many organizations and churches hang on to those past attitudes and values for one simple reason: The revolutionary process of change is agonizing. And working with mavericks involves risk taking of major proportions.

I have been amazed at the transformation of one of America's oldest and most stiffly bureaucratic institutions: General Electric. The maverick who led the charge was Jack Welch, who brought about—admittedly with much pain—the "new way" at GE. Jack Welch's goal was to transcend the old concepts of management itself. Instead of seeking better ways to control workers, Welch says he aimed to liberate them. As he explains, that goal is based on healthy self-interest:

> The old organization was built on control, but the world has changed. The world is moving at such a pace that control has become a limitation. It slows you down. You've got to balance freedom with some control, but you've got to have more freedom than you ever dreamed of. (Tichy and Sherman, *Control Your Destiny or Someone Else Will*, 20–21)

FINAL THOUGHTS

We were living in Southern California in 1987 during one of the region's biggest earthquakes. It occurred early in the morning and literally knocked me out of bed. That one morning shook loose most of my paradigms of safety. If anything is certain, it should be the ground beneath us, right?

Needless to say, I don't believe that anymore. We are living in times with earthquake-proportion change all around us. Sometimes it really scares me how fast the world is changing.

> Every few hundred years in Western history there occurs a sharp trans-formation. Within a few short decades, society rearranges itself.... Fifty years later, there is a new world. And the people born then cannot even imagine the world in which their grandparents lived and into which their parents were born. We are currently living through just such a tran-sition. (Peter Drucker, *Post-Capitalist Society*)

I especially plead with all of you who are in older institutions to aim for a flexible response to policies and procedures. If you're in senior man-agement or on the board and in control, take some risk and bring some fresh young blood into the equation. You will be amazed what a few new faces can bring to a stagnant group of people. Give them room to succeed.

We must avoid the danger that past communist regimes have made—they tried to make everyone equal, with no chance for true personal initia-tive. On my first trip to Russia in 1982, I was amazed when the tour guide pointed out that there was no unemployment in the land. I soon real-ized, as I studied the faces and learned the facts, that everyone had a job ... *but no one worked.* The system killed all possibility for personal initiative, and the results were—well, we know what happened to that approach.

> IN THE ABSENCE OF GREAT DREAMS, PETTINESS PREVAILS.

Don't allow your policies and procedures to stifle your brightest stars. Be flexible. Bend the rules if you believe that someone needs more space. Never be in bondage to your policy manual. Rules are made to be broken, principles are not. The best fighter pilot can change the rules of engagement, but he dare not violate the principles of gravity!

Don't allow nonessential pettiness to drive away the most promising young turks. Take risks and let people soar. Take this advice seriously: Goals should never arise out of corporate policy, company loyalty, or religious tradition alone.

Unless we're careful, we'll follow these four stages in the devolution of a fresh movement:

1. Men and women—every movement begins in the mind of one person.
2. Movement—when a new idea grows beyond the passion of just one person.
3. Machines—when a new idea becomes mechanistic/bureaucratic and begins to lose its original luster.
4. Monuments—when the passion for an idea dies, only monuments built to the original vision remain.

The key to arresting or reversing this trend is to allow for flexibility and constantly bring in fresh blood.

LEARN HOW TO RECOGNIZE TRULY USEFUL MAVERICKS

Not all troublemakers and malcontents are true mavericks. Some are just a pain to have around and don't do anyone much good. So it is important that we learn to recognize and reward properly the mavericks in our midst.

Legitimate mavericks who can bring you into the future:

➤ care not just for their own ideas but for the goals of the organization;

➤ are making a difference in their present position;

➤ are willing to earn the right to be heard;

➤ are influencing others and producing good results.

How to encourage the true mavericks who can help you:

➤ Give them a long tether—they need space to soar.

➤ Put them in charge of something they can really own.

➤ Listen to their ideas and give them time to grow.

➤ Let them work on their own if they wish.

➤ Leave them alone and give them time to blossom.

How to stifle the mavericks in your midst:

➤ Create as many layers of management as possible for decision making.

➤ Keep looking over their shoulders.

➤ Make your policy manual as thick as possible.

➤ Send everything to committees for deliberation.

➤ Make them wait.

Let me state this one last time: *Go for the mavericks.* Recruit them. Nurture them. Mentor them. For they bring us the future.

Organizations change of necessity and for a variety of reasons. But the single biggest impetus for change in an organization tends to be a new leader in a key job … someone with a fresh perspective who sees that the status quo is unacceptable. (John Kotter, *What Leaders Really Do*)

QUICK TIPS FOR LEADERS ON THE GO

No Room for Mavericks

They Bring Us the Future!

Big Idea: We use the word *maverick* here to connote *pioneer,* what Webster's dictionary describes as "an independent individual who does not go along with a group or party." The lifecycle of every organization seems to eventually move from passion to paralysis over time, and it is the pioneer spirit of a maverick that can save us. History is filled with many examples of innovators who were greatly misunderstood—but went on to create positive beneficial revolutions that changed the world. We have to learn how to recognize useful mavericks and make them a part of our teams.

➤ *Mavericks can save us from the slide toward institutionalism.* Over time our man made organizations grow old, rigid and tired, just like we humans do. The pioneering spirit of mavericks can stop that slide and turn it around.

➤ *Large organizations usually kill off mavericks before they can take root.* The larger and older an organization gets, the more it tends to reject creative types. We have to learn how to cultivate pioneers among us.

➤ *Mavericks make messes by their very nature—the good messes institutions need.* Institutions become too organized for their own good, and thus have a hard time accepting the disruption that change agents bring. These are the good messes we need to give ourselves a rebirth at middle age!

➤ *Learn to recognize truly useful mavericks.* Some people just love to complain, but there are useful mavericks who do not just cause trouble, but rather truly want to make a difference. We need to create space in our organizations for these beneficial mavericks to flourish.

DICTATORSHIP IN DECISION MAKING

5

Getting beyond
"I Know All the Answers"

- ➤ Dictators deny the value of individuals.
- ➤ The major players in any organization are like its stockholders: They should have a say in its direction.
- ➤ The one who does the job should decide how it is done.
- ➤ "Flat" organizations are the model of the future.

Dictatorships have their advantages. I spent most of the 1980s working in communist Eastern Europe, observing firsthand, countries such as Romania, East Germany, and Russia that were run by dictators. Life was quiet and predictable back then, especially when compared to the economic and political chaos that characterizes these same nations today. For decades all was calm and quiet in Eastern Europe, from Yugoslavia all the way to the eastern reaches of the Soviet empire bordering the Pacific: quiet, calm, and oppressed.

Dictatorships are like that. They take the fun out of life and break the human spirit that longs to soar with achievement. I can't begin to describe the dejected look of oppression I saw in the eyes of the common workers in Eastern Europe in those years. Crossing the borders in those days from western Europe into the East was like going from color TV to black-and-white. The gleam of joy and the fierce eyes of competition were rarely seen in whole generations that grew up in those times.

One of my greatest joys during those years of working in Eastern Europe was being in Berlin on November 9, 1989—to see, firsthand, the wall come down. I call it "history's greatest prison break." Freedom broke out everywhere. I think that the date of 11/9 changed the world as much or more (at least for the better) than 9/11! A change for the good of the human spirit and for millions of oppressed people who could now finally become leaders.

> "Take away my people but leave my factories and soon grass will grow on the factory floor. Take away my factories but leave my people and soon we will have a new and better factory."
> —Andrew Carnegie

Another label for the dictatorial style of leadership is what I call the "apostolic" view of decision making. This person believes that he or she has special knowledge or an anointing that gives him or her the inside edge on truth: "I know the answers, because I have been given special insight, knowledge, and position. Therefore, I will determine our direction, for I am the leader and I know best." It amazes me that such people even get into positions of power.

I recently ran into an old friend who told me of his recent experience working under a pastor who had this apostolic type of attitude. He ran his church as a corporate dictator would, making sure that every decision, large or small, was made only by him down to personally signing all the checks. He surrounded himself with the kind of yes-men who would submit to this domineering style. It became a miserable place to work, and my friend finally had the joy of retiring out of the misery. Not long after my friend left that church, the pastor crashed and burned in moral failure. Though he controlled everyone around him so completely, he apparently could not control his own passions.

In a very similar case, I received a call from a sheriff in Florida. At first I thought I was in trouble, but no, he was an elder in his church and had just read an earlier version of this book. All of the lay leaders in his church felt that the pastor was going in the wrong direction, and he wanted my advice. They were being smothered by a closed-minded leader. He asked me, "Are we right to oppose our pastor when we all disagree with him as one?" I advised him to try and reason with the leader as a group … with the wisdom of the many. The Bible says, "In the presence of many counselors there is wisdom." I take that to mean that the best direction for the whole is the collective wisdom of *all the leaders*. Unfortunately in this case, their pastor was not open to input.

Several times in my career, I have worked for bosses like that. After I had poured countless months of energy into a cause, my work would go up in smoke because the boss just decided that we were going to do something else. No dialogue—just dictatorship.

Don't be a jack-in-the-box leader. This is the person in charge who pops out of his box and declares, "It's been decided." Don't even think about uttering that phrase! It communicates that a decision was made behind closed doors that others had nothing to do with and that they can do nothing about. It deflates the human spirit like the mainsail going limp in the middle of a yacht race. All of a sudden, one feels dead in the water. The energies that were so focused before are suddenly nowhere to be found. In anger, most people will reply to that deadly phrase with, "Oh yeah? Who decided? Just let me get my hands on him!"

THE BEST OFTEN COMES FROM THE BOTTOM

At a recent employee briefing, I asked our team of sixty home office staff this question: "Where will the greatest ideas come from in our organization? Who will pioneer the greatest innovations? From what source will our great strides forward originate?" It was a trick question—I believed it was them! I went on to explain one of my fundamental beliefs about leadership: *The greatest ideas bubble up from the workers.* "They will come from you, not from me," I told them as they stared at me in disbelief. For some reason, I don't think anyone had ever told them that, and I'm not sure they believed me.

> "Fundamental values are not chosen from thin air based on the desires of executives, they are discovered within what already exists in an organization."
> —Jim Collins,
> *Built to Last*

We know by looking at history that the greatest strides forward in any field usually come from the "radical fringe," as opposed to the institutional core. I mentioned this in the last chapter as we looked at cultivating mavericks. Very seldom does the belly of an institution bring forth great bursts of creative energy and progress in a movement. Those on the fringes are the ones who usually come up with the best ideas. Look at the iPod, developed by a computer company and music outsiders! It single-handedly wiped out Sony, which had dominated the portable music market for decades with its Walkman portable CD players, and more recently with MP3 players.

An illustration from our kitchen shows how this principle works.

Having been brought up in a German home, one of the meals we often enjoyed as children was a dish called *griesbrei* (pronounced "GREASE-bry"). Because my parents didn't have much money when I was growing up, we had several meatless meals every week, one of them being griesbrei, which was basically souped-up Cream of Wheat. You bring the Cream of Wheat to a boil very slowly with milk, then add vanilla, eggs, and sugar. Once the porridge is done, you fold in whipped egg whites and serve it with milk, blueberries, and bananas. Because I have carried that tradition on to my children, they beg me to make griesbrei when they come home to visit.

How do you know when the griesbrei is ready? Huge bubbles begin to arise from the bottom, exploding on the surface. That is the magic signal.

What a great image that perfectly represents what my role as a leader is. It is to get those big bubbles to arise and burst forth on the surface of our organization. Those bubbles are the great ideas that I have to find hiding among the troops, maybe even at the bottom of the pot. A recent example comes from the world of branding. For a long time, all logo products, giveaways, and displays at WorldVenture were controlled by my office to assure that our brand message was consistent. But about a year ago, we hired some fresh blood in recruiting and I turned them loose on branding. Wow! I have never seen such cool stuff go out to the public with our logo. They are young, fresh,

Sydney J. Harris, on dictatorial bosses: "It is impossible to learn anything important about anyone until we get him or her to disagree with us; it is only in contradiction that character is disclosed. That is why autocratic employers usually remain so ignorant about the true nature of their subordinates."
—Field Newspaper Syndicate

and alive with ideas that I have never dreamed of considering. It reminded me again to avoid that desire to be an intellectual control freak. "Blessed are the control freaks, for they shall inhibit the earth!"

Dictators never make griesbrei. They never even turn the burner on. Their style is more akin to keeping the workers in the dark with the lid on the pot.

Thomas J. Watson Jr., the famous chairman of the board of IBM for many years, believed passionately that the best ideas would come from the fringes. He said, "Strangely, the expounders of many of the great new ideas of history were frequently considered on the lunatic fringe for some or all of their lives. If one stands up and is counted, from time to time one may get knocked down. But remember this: A man flattened by an opponent can get up again. A man flattened by conformity stays down for good."

FACILITATIVE LEADERSHIP

One big mistake dictators make is believing their own press reports. They think that the bigger they are, the more they know, and the more they should control others. In reality, leadership has more to do with influencing resources. The higher I move in leadership, the more resources I must manage. The greater the leader's responsibilities, the more he or she recognizes the intrinsic worth of the followers.

This is facilitative leadership. My job is to help those I lead release as much of their potential as possible. I do not do the work; others do it under my leadership. This is, in fact, a biblical approach to accomplishing the work of God on earth: "He gave some [leaders] as apostles, and some as prophets, and some as evangelists, and some as pastors and teachers, for the equipping [empowering] of the saints for the work of service" (Eph. 4:11–12 NASB). God never intended his earthly leaders to control their charges as dictators, but to equip them to do the work that must be done:

> To the elders among you, I appeal as a fellow elder.... Be shepherds of God's flock ... *not lording it over those entrusted to you,* but being examples to the flock.... *clothe yourselves with humility* toward one another, because,

> "God opposes the proud but gives grace to the humble."
> (1 Peter 5:1–3, 5, emphasis mine)

FLATTENING OUT THE ORGANIZATIONAL CHART

Let's talk organizational charts and see how this translates to paper. Chart A shows a typical organizational chart. It is based on the domineering model that puts someone at the top, controlling everything and everybody "below." This model does a great disservice, because it suggests that the more one goes "up" the organizational ladder, the more important one is and the more others are "under" that top leader responding to his or her commands.

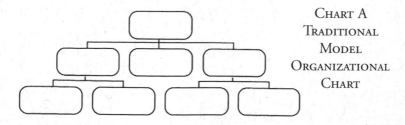

CHART A
TRADITIONAL
MODEL
ORGANIZATIONAL
CHART

Two alternate models I have observed are found in charts B and C. On the surface, chart B basically looks like chart A turned horizontally. But this illustrates the notion that a horizontal organizational structure is more efficient in releasing the potential of the workers scattered throughout the organization. I like this horizontal approach because it gives the idea of "leading the charge." I, as the leader, am at the front of the troops, leading them into battle, yet I am not viewed as the dictator who dominates from the top. The leader goes first, taking others with him or her, but is not viewed as being at the top of a mighty pyramid.

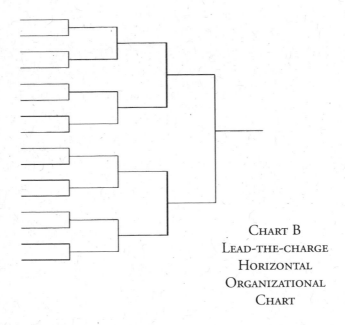

CHART B
LEAD-THE-CHARGE
HORIZONTAL
ORGANIZATIONAL
CHART

Chart C represents a flat networking model of organization, where the leader serves as a type of clearinghouse function between the various players or divisions of the group. Notice that there is communication and coordination not only between the leader and each of his or her key players but also among the key players themselves. The leader must not control all information as if he or she were a central switching station. I actually like chart C very much, and we at WorldVenture have moved toward this as we have put everyone in the organization on teams. Each of these circles represents a team. Leaders lead teams that fan out to other teams as the organization fans out around the world.

Chart D is a team-centered leadership structure where teams overlap in their tasks. This is probably more accurate than the stationary chart C, since lines of responsibilities usually overlap somewhat in all organizations. At times, we always get into each other's business! Where all the teams intersect at the center of this chart is where leadership happens. Not all teams come to the core of the organization either. Imagine a next level of circles emanating out from the first series as teams fan out.

A fifth organizational chart illustrates the servant-style leadership of Jesus Christ. In the inverted pyramid in chart E, everything rests on the shoulders of the leader. It's more of an attitude than anything else, where leaders realize that they are carrying the organization on their shoulders and that they need to make everyone else become successful.

As I have grown in my own leadership responsibilities, I have come to realize that I bear more and more of the burdens of more and more people. Recently someone commented to me, "It must feel great to be the leader of such a large organization." I chuckled as I shared with him that, in fact, it is not what it looks like from the outside. The higher you go in leadership, the more headaches you bear from other people's problems. I love the scene in the movie *Saving Private Ryan,* when Tom Hanks's character's unit asks him why they never hear him complaining about the lousy mission they are on to save Private Ryan. He responds, "I'm a captain, I don't gripe to my men. Gripes go up. Not down." You can be sure that the captain was carrying a huge burden of leadership on this mission ... he was figuratively, and sometimes literally, carrying every one of his men on his shoulders.

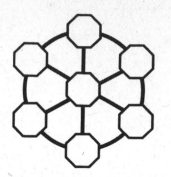

CHART C
FLAT
ORGANIZATIONAL
CHART

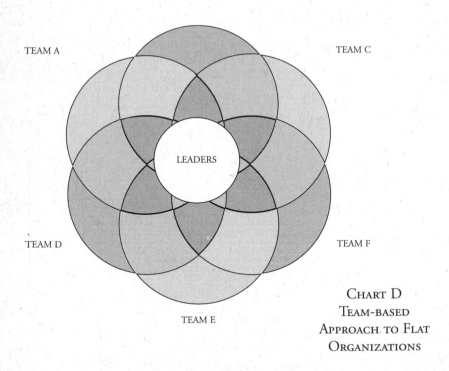

Chart D
Team-based
Approach to Flat
Organizations

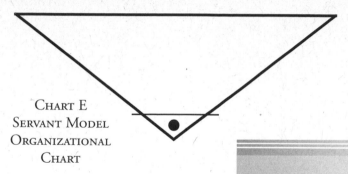

CHART E
SERVANT MODEL
ORGANIZATIONAL
CHART

DECISIONS BASED ON DIGNITY

Where I work we have developed a number of core values, which help determine our decision-making style. Two of the core values speak specifically to this issue of decision making and where ideas are going to come from:

Individual dignity. We diligently maintain and promote the dignity and worth of each individual within our organization worldwide. People with the proper sense of spiritual and emotional well-being are freed for productive ministry that is committed to goal-oriented planning and team accountability.

Corporate creativity. We encourage creative and innovative strategies

NEW STRUCTURES

There has evolved a new perspective on organizational structure. Trends in business and industry emphasize the flattening of administration, the creation of more fluid and changing teams to meet changing needs, and the embedding of responsibility, accountability, and authority at all levels. New theories of management tend to shy away from organizational charts and job descriptions that represent a top-down structure in which tasks are delegated downward, authority is tightly held, and micro-managing and monitoring of performance is important. A more appropriate model is an inverted triangle with an emphasis on supporting and enabling accomplishment.

—R. Daniel Reeves,
"Societal Shifts," *Ministry Advantage*

THE IDEAL SUPERVISOR

Here's the profile of an ideal supervisor developed by a group of supervisors participating in a training workshop on discipline at Brookdale Hospital Medical Center. Supervisors were asked to identify what they felt were ten major functions of an effective supervisor and to rank the functions in order of importance. Effective supervisors:

➤ delegate authority in areas affecting their work;

➤ consult with subordinates before making decisions pertaining to their job responsibilities;

➤ give employees the reasons for implementing decisions;

➤ don't play favorites;

➤ praise excellent work;

➤ reprimand subordinates who fail to observe the proper chain-of-command relationships;

➤ never reprimand or discipline in front of coworkers;

➤ encourage employees to offer their opinions and criticisms of supervisory policies;

➤ listen to employees' explanations before placing blame in disciplinary situations; accepts reasonable explanations, not excuses;

➤ obey all the rules that subordinates are expected to obey.

directed by the Spirit of God and implemented through policies and structures, which are characterized by mutual trust and cooperation.

In his book *Liberation Management,* Tom Peters emphasizes this strong new trend toward flat organizations. He has worked with many companies that are thriving in different industries and in different countries, and they all share one general characteristic: They are discarding the bureaucratic, hierarchical habits of the 1970s, '80s, and '90s. No longer are successful organizations using hierarchies and rule books to solve their basic problems. The old model was to use rule books to try to harness hundreds of thousands of "erratic, selfish human with a common purpose and to manage it in a predictable, scientific way. But those kinds of organizations become buried under their manuals and committees, having been left behind by their flat, lean rivals.

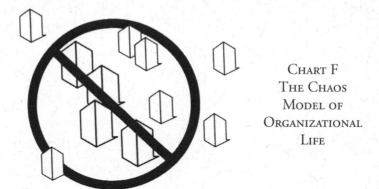

CHART F
THE CHAOS
MODEL OF
ORGANIZATIONAL
LIFE

One word of caution, however, on this issue of diplomacy and democracy in decision making: Don't throw out the baby with the bath water. An entirely leaderless organization is represented by chart F, the Chaos Model of Organizational Life. Some people today are advocating just such a model, but I think it only works well in some rare applications. In their book, *The Starfish and the Spider: The Unstoppable Power of Leaderless Organizations,* Ori Brafman and Rod Beckstrom look at how decentralization is changing many organizations. The title metaphor conveys the core concept: Though a starfish and a spider have similar shapes, their internal structure is dramatically different—a decapitated spider inevitably dies, while a starfish can regenerate itself from a single amputated leg. In the same way, decentralized organizations, like the Internet, the Apache Indian tribe, and Alcoholics Anonymous, are made up of many smaller units capable of operating, growing and multiplying independently of each other, making it very difficult for a rival force to control or defeat them (from a review in *Publishers Weekly,* October 5, 2006). This can make sense in some organizations, but it is my view that *few organizations are capable of successfully sustaining this type of existence for very long.*

Leaders should lead, not just implement consensus. When no one is in charge, chaos ensues. I firmly believe in the need for a single person to be in charge of each team in an organization, as opposed to a committee. Let's look at that concept next.

DICTATORS DON'T LEAD TEAMS

The alternative to dictatorship in decision making is team leadership. We have heard a lot about the team concept in the last couple of years. In our own organization, there is a strong movement among our field leadership staff to move toward a team emphasis. If I have heard the word *team* once from the fresh young recruits I have heard it a thousand times. The desire to work in a team environment goes hand-in-glove with the trend away from hierarchical, top-down organizational styles. Webster's defines *team* as "a number of persons associated together in work or activity; a number of persons selected to contend on one side in a match; a group of work-men each completing one of a set of operations." The word originated from the idea of a group of animals working together, as in two or more horses, oxen, or other draft animals harnessed to the same vehicle or plow. In our day we think of sports teams.

Our family had the joy of living in Chicago during the era of Michael Jordan and the Chicago Bulls. The Bulls won six world championships under the leadership of Jordan and their coach, Phil Jackson. No one doubts that Jordan was the leader of that team. But even Michael Jordan knows that the Bulls would never have won a championship without the strong support, energy, and talent of Coach Jackson and players like Horace Grant, Scottie Pippen, and John Paxson.

"What makes a good manager?" someone asked Yogi Berra. "A good ball club," Yogi replied.

I have listened to the cries for teams in our organization. And the move in that direction has been very healthy and productive. We have broken up the pieces of WorldVenture into teams everywhere, and I lead the executive leadership team, which consists of two other senior leaders, who report to me, and me. They, in turn, each have their own team to lead. Every leader has his or her team as the organization expands worldwide. There are teams at the home office, and teams out on the field. Though we have pushed most decision making far out to the staff, we still believe that the buck must stop somewhere for each major team, project, initiative, or department. Moving to teams has liberated management and harnessed the power of more and more creative energy at every level.

> "The leaders who work most effectively, it seems to me, never say 'I.' They don't think 'I.' They think 'we.' They think 'team.' They understand their job to be making the team function. They accept the responsibility and don't sidestep, but 'we' gets the credit. There is an identification (very often, quite unconscious) with the task and with the group. This is what creates trust, what enables you to get the task done."
> —Peter F. Drucker,
> *Managing the Non-Profit Organization: Principles and Practices*

Leadership is teamwork, coaching, creativity—and the synergy of a group of people inspired by their leader. No single person can corner the market on truth. I remember well a frustrating time in my own journey when I was deeply troubled by what I have called the apostolic style of leadership. I shared that story in my introduction. The apostolic style stands at the opposite end of the continuum from the leader who sees his primary role as managing the resources of a team. The apostle sees truth as having come down from on high. The apostle knows the battle plan and where the team will go. It is the team's responsibility to implement the dreams and visions that were singularly presented to the leader.

That approach may sound spiritual, but I don't believe it is biblical. The age of the apostles in the New Testament—men like Peter and Paul, who really did receive divine inspiration—is over. A leader's job today is to work together with his or her team, to draw out ideas and organize them. Unless there is goal ownership, there will never be strong support for the leader. The leader will ultimately have to steer the group into fulfilling the mission, but what that mission is should be determined together by the key players of the team.

> "You do not lead by hitting people over the head—that is assault, not leadership."
> —Dwight D. Eisenhower

In our organization, which we like to think is run as a Christian organization should be run, we rely on the guidance of God. We schedule times of prayer with our leadership team. I think we need to get serious with God if we expect him to get serious with us. We aren't perfect and don't always make the right decisions, but we have a history of good, solid organizational performance for many years. We as leaders *pray* together, *play* together, and do a lot of *talking* about the best course of action on any given decision.

DELEGATE DECISIONS WHENEVER POSSIBLE

Rather than always dictating decisions, a good leader will try as often as possible to let those he is leading make decisions. Insisting on being in on all the decisions communicates lack of trust and confidence. It also slows the development of new leadership. Very often, *how* a project is done doesn't really matter. If it is done differently but accomplished effectively, then the job gets done, which is all that matters.

I have certainly found this to work in our home. One of the Finzel family rules is "whoever is responsible to do the job can decide how it will be done." Of course we are interested in seeing the output, and we want to make sure the job is done correctly. But if I am in charge of cooking dinner tonight, then I would like to have the freedom of deciding what we will eat and how I will prepare it. Donna goes nuts if she watches me, so I send her out of the kitchen until dinner is served. It won't be done the way she does it, but she needs to relax, because I have been delegated that responsibility for the night. Actually, in our family we divide responsibilities on a week-by-week basis, according to the responsibilities of and pressures on the various family members during that week. And whoever does the job has the freedom to figure out how it will get done. From time to time my kids volunteer to wash my car. And you have to know that I obsess about having a very clean car inside and out. They don't wash my car the way I think it should be done, but I have learned to relax and accept their approach. They are saving me six dollars at the gas station! If I watch over their shoulders and constantly correct them, all I do is deflate their confidence.

Try delegating decisions throughout your organization. You will delight your staff. Just recently I had one of my managers come to me with a decision that needed to be made between two different options. He came to me saying, "You're the boss, and we need a decision." I could have taken one of two approaches. I could have given him the decision he wanted and he would have walked away and implemented my decision. But I want to empower him. Someday he may need to replace me, so he needs to have decision-making experience. The more I can push decisions into the various departments, the more ownership and enthusiasm there will be in implementing the decisions. So I asked the manager, "This is your area and you are the professional in this area, what is your gut-level opinion about which way we should go?"

His direction was not the way I would have gone, but I decided supporting his decision was more important than me getting my own way, so I told him to go with his intuition and I would back him. He walked away from that brief interchange feeling both valuable and important in this organization. And I walked away a winner, because I soon learned something new: I came to see that he was right and I was wrong!

Harry Truman, in his typical straightforward style, once said, "A leader is a person who has the ability to get others to do what they don't want to do, and like it." But we often have the uncomfortable feeling that leaders get us to do things for their own good and not for ours. We actually suspect we are being manipulated, but we follow anyway, because our jobs are on the line. Great leaders are those who truly feel that the led are just as important as the leader.

> "Leadership is the ability to recognize the special abilities and limitations of others, combined with the capacity to fit each one into the job where he will do his best."
> —J. Oswald Sanders, *Spiritual Leadership*

An effective leader in the new paradigm of shared leadership is Max De Pree. He sums up well the ideal of nondictatorial leadership: "Leadership is to be committed to a corporate concept of persons, the diversity of human gifts, covenantal relationships, lavish communications, including everyone, and believing that leadership is a condition of indebtedness" (Max De Pree, *Leadership Is an Art,* 72).

FINAL THOUGHTS

How dictators operate:

1. They hoard decisions.
2. They view truth and wisdom as primarily their domain.
3. They restrict decisions to an elite group.
4. They surprise their workers with edicts from above.

How facilitators lead:

1. They delegate decisions.
2. They involve others as much as possible.
3. They view truth and wisdom as being distributed throughout the organization.
4. They are developers.
5. They see people as their greatest resources for ideas that will bring success.
6. They give their people space to make decisions.
7. They let those who are responsible decide how jobs will be done.

When the best leader's work is done, the people will say, "We did it ourselves!"

QUICK TIPS FOR LEADERS ON THE GO

DICTATORSHIPS IN DECISION MAKING

Getting beyond "I Know All the Answers"

Big Idea: No one likes to live under dictators—they take all the fun out of life and work! Dictators in the business world hog all the decision-making. They feel that by virtue of their ownership, position, intelligence, or birthright, they are in charge of every key decision that will be made in the company or organization. These traditionalists do not see the value of facilitative leadership or the power of teams. Needless to say, dictators attract weak workers and cannot create a positive, empowering workplace.

➤ *Dictators deny the value of individuals.* The value of a dictator's organization resides at the top, not among the rank and file of its members. Dictators use people, they do not empower them.

➤ *The major players in any organization are like is stockholders*—they should have a say in its direction. Whether for a ministry or a business, every employee should have a sense of pride and ownership for the collective vision and passion of the company. The more ownership people sense, the more effort they will put forth for the group.

Everyone in the leadership community should have major input into direction and policy.

➤ *The one who does the job should decide how it is done.* The best management practice is to push decisions down to the people on the front lines. Let the people who are responsible for the outcome have as much ownership as possible in decision-making.

➤ *"Flat" organizations are the model of the future.* Though there are many ways to draw organizational charts, people today prefer to work in flat organizations without huge bureaucracies over their heads. Young workers especially prefer a shorter distance between the front lines and the CEO. Top down pyramids are a thing of the past!

6

DIRTY DELEGATION

Refusing to Relax and Let Go

➤ Overmanaging is one of the great cardinal sins of poor leadership.

➤ Nothing frustrates those who work for you more than sloppy delegation with too many strings attached.

➤ Delegation should match each worker's follow-through ability.

It happened again yesterday. (Beware the confessions of a dirty delegator.) I decided that we would run a full-color half-page ad in an upcoming magazine for a special promotion. I called in Ted, my communications director, whose department is responsible for such things, and asked him to go to work on some ideas for me to consider. He went off, charged with a new project for the boss, not knowing that I was about to cut him off at the knees with my next move.

At about the same time I gave Ted this assignment, I met a brand consultant who wanted to do some work for us. His portfolio impressed me, so I told him about the ad project and asked him if they did these kinds of projects. "Sure, it's our specialty," he responded. I asked him to go to work on the ad, "just for ideas," and soon received a fax from him with a great concept for the ad.

Guess what came next … Ted called me into his office to show me the ad he had come up with. He had obviously put a great deal of work into the project. He had even gone down to the local library to scan ads in magazines similar to the one we were creating the ad for. "Ted," I told him with fear and trembling, "it's pretty good, but I have decided to go with the consultant's concept for the ad." Hindsight is 20/20, and I realized that he had not even been aware that he was competing with someone else.

> ### DELEGATION WORKS FOR YOU
>
> "I'd rather get ten men to do the job than to do the job of ten men."
> —D. L. Moody

How do you think Ted felt? How would you have felt? The issue is not who did the best job on the ad. The issue is that I did not tell Ted that someone else was competing with him for the concept. I gave him the project, and then I took it back from him. And that is what dirty delegation is all about.

WHY LEADERS FAIL TO DELEGATE

Snoopy is lying on top of his famous dog house. He is complaining in a whining puppy voice that everyone demands something from him. He has so much more to do than he can possibly get accomplished. In the final frame of the cartoon, Snoopy sighs, "I hate being head beagle!"

Being head beagle would be a lot easier if we could learn to spread out the work to other competent workers around us. But most leaders find it hard to let go of their precious responsibilities. They overestimate the value of being the top beagle, and they underestimate the value of their followers. In fact, no leadership problem is a greater challenge than learning the fine art of clean delegation. And few leadership hang-ups create more defeated spirits as in the case I just described.

> ## WHY LEADERS DON'T DELEGATE
>
> ➤ Fear of losing authority
> ➤ Fear of work being done poorly
> ➤ Fear of work being done better
> ➤ Unwillingness to take the necessary time
> ➤ Fear of depending on others
> ➤ Lack of leadership training and positive delegation experience
> ➤ Fear of losing value in the organization

There are many reasons delegation is hard to do well:

Fear of losing authority. It takes a great deal of faith to have the courage to turn important work over to others. Those who are especially hung up with the old model of control will have a tough time learning how to delegate cleanly. Dictators never delegate, they just look for the weak-willed person who can implement their every desire.

Fear of work being done poorly. This is the most obvious reason why some leaders just can't bring themselves to delegate. There is fear that the responsibility will be handled poorly. In some cases such fears are justified—as when a heart surgeon trusts only a few nurses to assist in the stress of intricate bypass surgery. But often there is simply the hang-up of not being willing to allow others to do the work their way. In many cases, however, there is no perfect way to do the job, as long as the job gets done.

Fear of work being done better. On the flip side, some leaders are paranoid about having subordinates show them up and do a better job than they themselves could have done. This is a sad display of pride that will eventually ruin a leader's effectiveness. Our goal is to develop new leaders who will eventually replace us (more on that in chapter 9), so we shouldn't worry about others having skills better than our own. If you honestly believe that the best ideas flow up from below, then you must believe that some of the rank-and-file workers will do some work better than you. A leader should surround himself or herself with specialists who can each do their particular job better than their supervisor.

Unwillingness to take the necessary time. Delegation takes time. Task-oriented people just want to get the job done; their impatience precludes waiting on others to do the job. They think, *I can do the job better and faster if I do it myself. If I take the time to delegate, I first have to meet with the person and explain what I want. Then I have to wait for them to have the time to do the project … and I have to hope that when I finally get the job back, it will be up to my standards!*

Fear of depending on others. This problem comes right on the heels of the impatience just described. It is the issue of leadership independence, which some people find very hard to relinquish. They are so independent and so aggressive that they cannot learn to depend on others in a team environment, in which the whole task is completed when each member does his or her part.

> "The best executive is the one who has sense enough to pick good men to do what he wants done, and self-restraint enough to keep from meddling with them while they do it."
> —Theodore Roosevelt

Lack of leadership training and positive delegation experience. Perhaps for some leaders, they have never been trained in the fine art of delegating. No one has shown them how, no one has ever believed in them enough to delegate to them, so they have learned to work as independents doing their own work. If this is your experience, then you should begin with small experiments at delegating tasks to others that you would normally handle yourself. Try it, and see how you can multiply your effectiveness!

Fear of losing value in the organization. We all want to feel needed, and one of the problems of good delegation is that there may not be as much for you to do. And for many people, that translates into loss of value. "If *I* don't do it, I am not needed!" It's simply not true. The value of the leader is to coach and lead, not to micromanage.

DELEGATION ENABLES PERSONAL OWNERSHIP

As we have seen, some of the greatest lessons of poor leadership come from the ineptitude of communist regimes before the fall of the Iron Curtain. This is particularly true in this issue of delegation. Delegation is about private ownership of one's work, and in the communist system, there simply was no private ownership. No one took pride in his or her work, and therefore, nothing got accomplished. After seventy years of communism, you find in former communist nations a completely failed infrastructure that is impossible to rebuild. I feel sorry for those millions who are paying the price today for the decades of tyranny that denied men and women the simple freedom to own their work and pursue their passions through private enterprise.

To illustrate the power of personal ownership of private property, take the example of how food was produced in the former Soviet Union. More than 90 percent of farming was done on collective farms, but those farms produced only 10 percent of the food consumed. Crops on the collective farms rotted in the fields, because there was no one to harvest them. One Iowa farmer who owns his own land could outproduce a collective farm that employed hundreds of workers on land many times larger. Why? Pride of ownership and personal control.

Where did the bulk of the Soviet Union's best food come from? Some, of course, was imported from the West, including yearly doses of wheat from the good old Midwestern farmers of America. But almost half of the fresh food supply for the population came from tiny private plots that citizens were allowed to own. Those little plots rimmed the perimeters of many Russian cities. With every spare minute, private citizens worked those parcels as the only real expression of what they were able to accomplish beyond the all-encompassing reach of the government.

> ## THE FOUR STAGES OF DELEGATION
>
> 1. Assignment
> 2. Authority
> 3. Accountability
> 4. Affirmation

In the same way, we must give our workers freedom to own their work, or they will lose the pride of personal accomplishment and their productivity will quickly wane.

HOW TO TAKE THE WIND OUT OF THEIR SAILS

Overmanaging is one of the greatest sins of leadership. We must be careful not to micromanage people to death. Delegation means giving people the freedom to decide how jobs will be done. Dirty delegation constantly looks over the shoulders of those asked to do the work. It is confining and restricting to the creativity and problem-solving potential that longs to come out of most people. It often results in decisions made behind the backs of those to whom the work was delegated.

"OK, Sam. Here is what I want you to do," our boss said to my good friend, who was new on the scene in this particular organization. "You're bright. Study this problem, and come up with a solution that we can use to fix it."

That's all Sam wanted to hear. He was like a hungry dog that had just been tossed a fresh steak. He tackled the assignment with all the gusto you could expect from an eager young recruit. He dug in, turned on, rolled up his sleeves, and went to work. Among the many things running through his mind, Sam wanted to (a) make a great impression by showing his boss that he was even brighter than rumored, and (b) get off to a great start by helping solve a major challenge that had been plaguing us for months. He studied and researched the problem, explored possible options, and over the next months pounded out an impressive report on his keyboard. I recall the final product being close to fifty pages.

Sam had been given a long lead time to complete the project. When it was finally finished, the fateful day came for him to deliver his first work of art to his new boss. With great pride and a sense of fulfillment he placed the document in the boss's in-box. And he waited … and waited … and waited. Hearing nothing after several days, he finally got the courage to stop his boss in the hallway and ask him about the report. "Looks good, Sam," he said almost off-the-cuff, "but we've decided to take another approach with that project."

What? Did he hear what he thought he heard? You could hear the air rushing out of his bubble as his ego completely deflated. To say that Sam was crushed, angered, and puzzled would be to put it mildly. How would you have reacted? Can you feel the rage that Sam felt that day? How many mistakes did this

> ### FOUR QUESTIONS EVERY FOLLOWER ASKS:
>
> 1. What am I supposed to do?
> 2. Will you let me do it?
> 3. Will you help me when I need it?
> 4. Will you let me know how I'm doing?
>
> —Dr. Lorne Sonny, *The Business Ministry Journal*

leader make with Sam? I can think of several outrageous ones, including the following:

Lack of empathy for the enlisted folks. The longer you lead, the less you remember what it was like to follow. For some there may have never been a chance to really feel what followers feel. People who hold great power in organizations usually don't sense their power—like a skunk that's immune to his own aroma! Leaders lead ... and followers cringe!

Failure to "give" work to others. This leader never really "gave" the project to Sam at all. He teased Sam like you would tease a dog with a bone that you have no intention of giving him. He showed a great lack of respect by giving Sam the project and then taking it back without ever bothering to let him know. Any assignment should be given with the authority and freedom to complete the task in whatever way an employee sees fit. And further, follow-up procedures should be implemented out of respect for the dignity of that worker. Any person who puts time and effort into an endeavor would like to hear of the outcome.

Failure to stay in touch. The next classic mistake Sam's boss made is that he never bothered to check up on how Sam was doing. Had he known how Sam was killing himself to do this project right, he would have seen the sense of ownership that had taken over Sam's emotions, and he would have been tuned in to the problem that was looming on the horizon.

Short-circuiting the decision-making process. Sam was simply out of any loop in the decision-making process. In fact, once a decision about the project was made, he wasn't even informed.

But he was not alone, for no communication system was in place for people to know when big decisions were made behind closed doors. We will discuss this further when we talk about communication chaos in chapter 7.

Playing the inner-circle game. Who really made the decision about scuttling Sam's project? The boss and his private inner circle of top management. I've seen quite a few organizations—even Christian ministries—that pride themselves on running a biblically centered operation while in reality they hold a double standard when it comes to information flow.

They boast equality and transparency in the fellowship of the family of faith, but in fact keep many parts of that family in the dark. I know that certain information must be kept confidential, but that is not the problem here. Sam never got an honest hearing. The boss and his inner circle decided that they knew the answers they wanted before the project came to fruition.

By the way, what do you think this incident did to Sam's enthusiasm? Yes, it took all the wind out of his sails. He tossed out the respect he had for this leader, and he crawled into a shell that he maintained until the day he resigned not too many years later. From that day on, he decided that his number-one goal in the organization was his own self-preservation—not the good of the whole. He told me, and I quote, "I will never volunteer to do a project for him again. Period."

THE GREAT DELEGATION

Delegation is seen throughout the Bible. When I think of delegation in the Bible, I think of the great leader Nehemiah and the thousands of workers to whom he delegated responsibilities as they rebuilt the walls of Jerusalem. Then there was Aaron, brother of Moses, who was put in charge of the camp while Moses spent extended time in the presence of God on Mount Sinai. Aaron is a good example of delegated responsibility gone bad, for he failed in his duties and Moses came back to a mess. That is the risk we take when we delegate.

In the New Testament we read about the greatest task ever delegated to a group of leaders. Jesus delegated to his disciples the fulfillment of the

Great Commission—spreading the word about God's love. He prepared them well and then turned them loose. Due to their success, many of you who are reading these words are followers of that message. Notice how Jesus Christ passed on his authority to his disciples:

> All authority in heaven and on earth has been given to me. Therefore go and make disciples of all nations, baptizing them in the name of the Father and of the Son and of the Holy Spirit, and teaching them to obey everything I have commanded you. And surely I am with you always, to the very end of the age. (Matt. 28:18–20)

Jesus not only gave them an important job to do, he promised to follow up on that delegation with his presence: "Surely I am with you always." He was going to hold his followers accountable, but he also intended to encourage them along the way. Excellent practice of delegation!

After just three short years of preparation, Jesus was counting on his disciples to fulfill the mandate of his revolution to the ends of the earth. He trusted them so completely that he had no backup plan. Either they would build the church and start a worldwide movement … or it just would not happen. There was no secret division of his enterprise lying behind closed doors that he was waiting to break out at just the opportune moment.

I think the twelve disciples knew that they were it, and that Jesus believed in them so completely that he had no other plan. Thus they gave themselves to the Great Commission with reckless abandon and devotion, even to the point of death. It is amazing what followers will do for the leader who shows this level of faith in them.

In the second generation of Christ's followers, the apostle Paul stands out as again seeing the importance of delegating. Near the end of his life,

Paul laid out his delegation strategy for completing the task of building the New Testament church. He counted on a young leader named Timothy:

> You then, my son, be strong in the grace that is in Christ Jesus. And the things you have heard me say in the presence of many witnesses entrust to reliable men who will also be qualified to teach others. (2 Tim. 2:1–2)

Paul is asking those to whom he delegated the task of spreading the gospel to delegate it down the line to a third and fourth layer of individuals. That is good delegation—passing the authority and responsibility throughout the enterprise.

Follow-through Styles That You Should Know

An important principle that many leaders stumble on is the need to recognize that different kinds of followers need different styles of supervision. Once I have delegated a responsibility, I must practice various forms of supervision and accountability according to the condition of the follower.

I can best explain the difference with illustrations of two very different people I delegate work to and how they respond. One is named Andrew, my youngest son. The other is named Joe, and he is decades older and wiser.

Andrew falls on the low end of what I call the delegation continuum (see chart). I have been training him and our other kids on "KP" in our family. *KP* stands for "kitchen police," and our four children have a rotating system: on certain days of the week each has KP. At least that's the theory! The responsibilities include such things as setting the table for dinner, clearing the table after dinner, and taking out the garbage. Andrew has very low motivation, interest, or skill for this job, and thus, I have to constantly hover over him to get him to do it. What teenager loves to help in the kitchen? Not only do I have to constantly remind him to do his work, but I also have to help him and demonstrate how. If I leave him alone, the chances are high that the system will break down. Andrew needs close and constant supervision of a very specific nature. Some people who work with and for you will be in the same category.

Then there is Joe, who has worked for me for more than a year on a very demanding special project for our organization. I live in Denver where our headquarters are, and he lives in California, far away from my daily personal supervision. But that's no problem, because Joe is the ultimate self-directed worker—he gets the job done on autopilot. He never misses deadlines and does fabulous work. What is the difference between Andrew and Joe? Not just age, but *motivation, interest,* and *skill.*

This practice of varying your style of supervision according to your followers' follow-through style could be called situational leadership. One of the best books I have read on the fine art of delegating and supervising is Hersey, Blanchard, and Johnson's *Management of Organizational Behavior.* They introduce the concept of situational leadership and show that there are four ways of delegating and keeping up with those to whom work has been assigned, based on their maturity and motivation. These four leadership alternatives are delegating, participating, selling, and telling. The greatest mistake we can make in supervising is to treat everyone the same. Hersey and Blanchard describe these four different supervision styles thusly:

Delegating. This is the best kind of supervision for the person who, like Joe, is self-directed and highly skilled at his or her work.

Participating. This is the kind of situation in which the leader is working with the follower. The leader literally shows the follower how to get the job done. When I taught my oldest son how to cut our lawn, the first season we did it together. Now he can do it totally on his own while I am out of town. I moved with him from the participating to the delegating category.

Selling. Here the people have high skill but low motivation. They will do the job best if you can sell them on doing it. This is something we who work in nonprofit organizations must practice day in and day out.

Telling. This is the approach I take with Andrew and my other children, since they have low interest, low motivation, and low skill in the kitchen. With some people, you must strongly tell them that they must do a job whether they like it or not. This is the lowest form of delegation and should be used as little as possible.

THE DELEGATION CONTINUUM:
THE FOLLOW-THROUGH STYLES OF DIFFERENT WORKERS

Low Interest	High Interest
Low Motivation	High Motivation
Low Skill	High Skill

Telling ------------- Selling ------------ Participating ------------- Delegating

LET'S PLAY "PASS THE MONKEY"

In the 1950s, *The Harvard Business Review* ran an article about delegation and monkeys, from which the expression arose, "get that monkey off my back." In that fascinating account, the writer described a typical scenario that is repeated daily in our office and in organizations around the world. Every time you give a job to someone, picture yourself putting a monkey on his or her back. It is their responsibility to care for and feed that monkey until it's time to set it free—that is, until the task is completed. It sounds simple, but it's not. A coworker comes into my office with a problem about a responsibility that has been delegated to him or her. There seems to be a snag, and the person needs help. Their goal is to get the monkey off his or her back and onto mine. How does the monkey jump on *my* back? By my saying something like, "Well, let me give it some thought," "I'll see what I can do," "Let me talk to some others about it," or the worst response, "I'll take care of it." In each case I've relieved the person of his or her monkey. I have taken responsibility for its care and feeding.

> "If everything seems under control, you are not going fast enough."
> —Mario Andretti

If this process repeats itself several times a day, your back will be overburdened and the noise unbearable. I have a back full of monkeys that are really the responsibilities of other people. I am happy to have an open-door policy and help colleagues problem solve. But I have an imaginary sign over my doorway as you look out of my office that reads, "Did they take their monkey with them?"

Don't do other people's work for them. That is my natural temptation, like when I ask my children to do a job that I would normally do myself. I must cultivate greater independence and responsibility in both of us by giving them a job and allowing them do it. Not long ago I asked my son to wash my car after school. He was looking forward to it, but, to his dismay, I arrived home that evening with a newly washed vehicle.

"What happened, Daddy?" he asked with great surprise and disappointment. I had to confess to him that I was practicing dirty delegation again. I figured it was easier to run it through the car wash on the way home than to have him take an hour and do an inferior job. In that case, I preferred the easier route to setting the monkey free, and simultaneously, didn't follow through on my request of my son. By not entrusting him, he may have lost trust in me.

FINAL THOUGHTS

This issue of delegation is an issue of respect. With responsibility must come the authority to do a job. I believe in the 80/20 rule of success. Eighty percent of the time I'll make the right decision, and 20 percent of the time I will make mistakes or not do something as well as it could have been done. I allow my subordinates the freedom of the 80/20 rule as well and give them grace and room to fail.

My rule of thumb is this: He who is asked to do the job plans how it will be done. We can check our workers' progress, but we should not (a) constantly look over their shoulders, (b) tell them how to do their work, (c) reject their work in favor of our "expert" approach, or (d) reverse their strategy decisions simply for ones we might favor as leaders.

Key Ingredients for Clean Delegation:

1. Have *faith* in the one to whom you delegate.
2. *Release* the desire to do it "better" yourself.
3. *Relax* from the obsession that it has to be done your way.
4. Practice *patience* in the desire to do it faster yourself.
5. *Vision* to develop others by delegating.

Guidelines for Clean Delegation:

1. Choose qualified people.
2. Exhibit confidence.
3. Make their duties clear.
4. Delegate the proper authority.
5. Do not tell them how to do the work.
6. Set up accountability points along the way.
7. Supervise according to their follow-through style.
8. Give them room to fail occasionally.
9. Give praise and credit for work well done.

QUICK TIPS FOR LEADERS ON THE GO

DIRTY DELEGATION
Refusing to Relax and Let Go

Big Idea: Dirty delegation follows right on the heals of dictatorship in decision making. It is all about refusing to let go of control. A person who delegates well gives people a job to do and the responsibility and freedom to see the job through. Dirty delegators constantly watch workers over their shoulders and cannot relax and let go of the task.

> ➤ *Overmanaging is one of the great cardinal sins of poor leadership.* Leaders who cannot let go of delegated projects are insecure. They worry that no one can do the job as well as they can. Ultimately their hang up is that they don't believe in the abilities of other people.

> ➤ *Nothing frustrates those who work for you more than sloppy delegation with too many strings attached.* Giving an employee a job without the space to complete it is demeaning. This behavior communicates to an employee that he or she is a child who cannot be trusted. No one enjoys working in this type of smothering environment, and there is no way that the people in this situation can grow.

➤ *Delegation should match each worker's follow-through abil-ity.* As leaders, we have to learn the capacity and abilities of the people who work for us. We must learn who we can trust with responsibilities. Those who are faithful with a little should be given ever greater tasks to manage.

7

COMMUNICATION CHAOS

Singing from the Same Page in the Hymnal

➤ Never assume that anyone knows anything.
➤ The bigger the group, the more attention must be given to communication.
➤ When left in the dark, people tend to dream up wild rumors.
➤ Communication must be the passionate obsession of effective leadership.

I remember the summer that we introduced our children to Yellowstone National Park for the first time. I had not been there myself since I was a child and had forgotten how vast America's most famous national park really is. Amid the beauty of Yellowstone was one sad blemish that shocked us: the many scars of forest fires that destroyed much of the park in 1989.

And in those ashes was the story of a communication disaster that almost caused more damage than the fire itself.

It seems that the employees of the private company that runs the concessions in Yellowstone became worried for their lives during the height of the fires that threatened to ravage the entire park that summer. As the fires grew more and more dangerous, a rumor began to circulate that the executives of the concession company had a secret escape plan to get out of danger if the fires got too close. Information spread that the employees would have to fend for themselves, and it wasn't long before the company had a near mutiny on its hands, since it was seen as taking care of itself first and employees second, if at all.

Lack of communication about evacuation plans coupled with the unfounded rumor destroyed confidence in the company's goodwill. After learning of the problem, the company hired a forest service spokesman who brought daily updates on the status of the fire to all employees. Included in the communications was a detailed explanation of evacuation plans that all employees were a part of. The company had no executive escape plan, and the leadership had fully intended to make sure that every employee was safe amid the disaster. But that was not communicated, so the employees were left to speculate.

Rumor mills are part and parcel of every work group. Rumors often spread like a forest fire, and rarely, if ever, are they anywhere close to reality. Perhaps it was foolish for those Yellowstone concession employees to believe such a heartless rumor, but when things get bad and survival is involved, people can begin to create their own reality if the true reality is not communicated.

Never assume that anyone knows anything. This is a core leadership principle. We can never communicate enough in our organizations. Like the pulsing red cells rushing through our veins keeping our bodies alive, communication systems are the lifeblood of organizations. The folks at the furthest extremities desperately need to know what is going on in the minds of those at the leadership center, if they are to feel comfortable, safe, and knowledgeable about their work. In his excellent book, *The Four Obsessions of an Extraordinary Executive,* Patrick Lencioni states that two of the four obsessions have to do with communication: organizational clarity and overcommunication of that clarity. Organizational clarity is "the basic definition of what the company does. As simple as this seems, it is common to encounter employees in most companies who are not sure how to describe or define the organization's basic mission" (159).

Though much of my job as a CEO is communicating our vision and selling our dream out among the public constituents, my insiders need to hear from me just as much, if not more. In fact, I expend as much energy on internal as on external communications. I never assume anymore that even my closest associates can read my mind—I've learned too much from watching false information spread.

HOW TO KNOW YOU HAVE A COMMUNICATION HANG-UP

A gentleman was walking down a residential street and noticed a man struggling with a washing machine at the doorway of his house. When he volunteered to help the homeowner was overjoyed, and the two men together began to work and struggle with the bulky appliance. After several minutes of fruitless effort, the two stopped and just looked at each other. They were on the verge of total exhaustion. Finally, when they caught their breath, the first man said to the homeowner, "We'll never get this washing machine in there!" To which the homeowner replied, "In? I'm trying to move it out!"

Communication chaos begins when small groups start getting larger.

THE LIFE CYCLES OF ORGANIZATIONS

Birth   Adolescence   Maturity

→

COMMUNICATION PATTERNS
Oral	Written
Informal	Formal
Spontaneous	Planned
Active	Passive
Lively	Liturgical

As long as the organization is small, oral communication is sufficient and generally everyone knows everything. But as things grow larger, the need for more formal communication grows. You'll recall the chart from chapter 4 on the life cycles of organizations. I have included it again here in a slightly different form. I have displayed the process from birth to maturity, without the decline toward death. As organizations grow from small entrepreneurships into professionally managed organizations, communication must be given more attention and must become more formal.

Early in my career, I had the exciting opportunity to be in on the ground floor of starting a new leadership training organization based in Vienna, Austria. We were a group of zealous entrepreneurs who were creating something out of nothing. Only five families were involved at the outset, and we started out in borrowed space in the basement of an office building. I remember vividly how we would make decisions in the hallways and communicate orally from one open office door to the other. In fact, we would all go jogging together in the Vienna woods and plan our strategy for the next six months. It was exciting, it was passionate, and it all happened so quickly! We never bothered writing down any of the great stuff we were cooking up, because we were all there. That approach worked great, and we were off and running. There was no question about which page of the hymnbook we were singing from.

But five years down the road, we had grown to a staff of more than sixty and had taken over the entire building. The organization had taken on a life of its own. The style of decision making that worked so easily at first now created chaos and frustration throughout the organization. "Hallway decision making" became the negative label for poor communication. That which had worked so well informally now had to be formalized. There was massive confusion everywhere about what we were trying to do, what our priorities were, and the details of operational strategy. Inspiration was replaced with uncertainly and misunderstanding—the fun was gone.

One reason the informal broke down was that newcomers to the group were left in the dark. Some of them hated jogging! The same small band kept making all the decisions orally, and no paper trail was left for others to trace.

The very passion that surrounds a young upstart can kill it in adolescence. As organizations grow, the original group of founders can become an inside elite. Since they were there from the beginning, they have the most information and power. Newcomers feel left out and in the dark. I recall one of the new employees in our group complaining about the lack of information in this vivid fashion: "I feel like I'm living on a mushroom farm—I'm left completely in the dark and fed manure from time to time." That was a revealing statement of the kind of pain that can be caused by poor communication. Patrick Lencioni goes on to state in *Four Obsessions,*

Within companies that effectively overcommunicate, employees at all levels and in all departments understand what the organization is about and how they contribute to its success. They don't spend time speculating on what executives are really thinking, and they don't look for hidden messages among the information they receive. As a result, there is a strong sense of common purpose and direction, which supersedes any departmental or ideological allegiances they may have. (166)

EXACTLY WHERE ARE WE GOING?

Orchestra conductors have the unique ability to bring harmony out of chaos. For a decade, Donna and I had the joy of living in Vienna, one of the world's greatest music capitals. What a privilege it was. One of the highlights of our social life was to go to the Philharmonic Hall and enjoy the beautiful Vienna Philharmonic Orchestra. Musicians consider the hall where the Philharmonic meets to be the most acoustically perfect music hall anywhere in the world. And I don't know of a better symphony orchestra than the Vienna Philharmonic. However, when the orchestra first comes out and begins tuning, their sounds amaze you by their discord and chaos. How can this noise become beautiful music? The answer lies in the conductor. He walks out onto the stage, steps onto his platform, taps his music stand, and gives the artists the A note. All of his leadership is wrapped up in that A note, where harmony flows out of chaos.

> "The words *information* and *communication* are often used interchangeably, but they signify quite different things.
> Information is *giving out;* communication is *getting through.*"
> —Sydney J. Harris,
> Publishers-Hall Syndicate

About five years into our project in Vienna, we were beginning to sense growing pains. We invited a management consultant to come in and spend a day with our top leadership. We sat in a circle around a large conference room table and began to talk about fundamentals of the organization.

The consultant asked us each to write down the core purpose of our organization. Then we went around the circle and read what we had written. Not two of us said the same thing, and some were far afield from the others! No wonder there was so much chaos among us! Like the strings of a guitar that lose their tuning, we had lost our harmony as a leadership group. You know you're in trouble when your top leadership is confused about such fundamental issues as the core purpose for the group's existence!

Our underlying problem was the failure to make the shift from an oral planning mode to a more formal written one. It was time we sharpened our strategic plan in writing, so we could all sign off on it and could then use that body of knowledge to orient each new member of the group. When the group is small, everyone knows the score, because everyone has time to touch base with each other almost daily. But if your group grows, you as the leader cross a threshold where you can no longer physically stay in touch through informal means. In our case, we began to have people in other cities and countries as parts of our organization. There was no way that the oral tradition could continue to drive the operation. It wasn't much fun, but we had to get the organization on paper if we were going to thrive in the long run.

Sooner or later you must put your plans down in writing and spell out your direction clearly. That doesn't mean that the plans won't change, but it does mean that everyone knows the rules of the game. It means that you're all trying to conquer the same mountain.

COMMUNICATION: A SERIES OF LINKAGES

The higher you go in leadership, the more sensitive you have to be about everything you communicate. I call this becoming aware of "communication linkages." Every time I make a phone call or write a letter or make a decision, I have to ask, "What people are affected by this decision/letter/memo/directive? What are the linkages?" It can drive me crazy to think of all the people who need to be informed when a decision is made. Sometimes I feel like a fly caught in a spider web, tangled and stuck because of all the sticky communication lines attached to me! But I know that the consequences of not informing everyone are communication chaos and damaged relationships. Invariably, I send copies of memos or letters to various other people to make sure they are aware of my decisions and actions.

When meetings are over, the hard work of communication begins. It's called "cascading communication," the flow of information that has to occur as soon after leaders make decisions as possible. Picture it like ripples in a pond after you cast in a stone. The stone is the decision; the ripples are the cascades of information that move out quickly. In his book, *Death by Meeting,* Patrick Lencioni challenges leaders to make sure that within twenty-four hours of a meeting every person affected by the outcome be informed.

Not only must you communicate clearly the decision you make, quite often you must clear those decisions with a number of colleagues before finalizing them. Even though I have authority to make decisions in my organization, I would damage the entire system by unilaterally doing so without conferring with the key individuals involved.

Let me give a case in point. We have a gentleman who has been working for us for more than thirty-five years in Manila. Just five years short of retirement, he is looking for a new challenge. I am very interested in deploying him to Moscow to help us develop our work in that part of the world, which is booming with new opportunities. This is what I call internal recruitment, where an insider is recruited from one part of the organization to work in another.

He went to Moscow this past summer, to test the waters, and explore possibilities. He came back exuberant and excited. However, I cannot unilaterally redeploy him without taking into account his previous supervisor who oversaw his work in the Philippines, and his potential new supervisor who oversees our work in Europe. The entire process must be coordinated with all of the principal parties involved. And that is the hard work of effective communication.

WHEN NEW LEADERS CHANGE THE RULES

There is never a time when more in-house communication is needed than when a new leader arrives on the scene. People need to know what to expect of their new leader. If you are that person, make sure you over-communicate as an obsession. If you are living under new leadership, demand to hear from the leader as much as possible about their dreams and visions for the group. When I became CEO of WorldVenture fifteen years ago, it meant taking over an organization that had been run with a dramatically different leadership style for twenty-two years. I was as different from my predecessor as a carrot is from a pickle. Not only were our styles dramatically different, but I was also from a younger generation. A boomer taking over from a builder. How did that play with our staff? It made them very uneasy and nervous, because they didn't know what to expect. For the first couple of years, the jury was out on whether

THE COMMUNICATION LIFE BLOOD

"A corporation's values are its life's blood. Without effective communication, actively practiced, without the art of scrutiny, those values will disappear in a sea of trivial memos and impertinent reports. There may be no single thing more important in our efforts to achieve meaningful work and fulfilling relationships than to learn and practice the art of communication."
—Max De Pree, *Leadership Is an Art*

I would survive, and the number-one question everyone wanted to know was, "Who is this new kid on the block?" I survived and thrived by a passionate commitment to face time and open communication. Communication became a supremely important part of my new job, just like when a new coach takes over. The team has the right to know how they're going to play ball.

EFFECTIVE LEADERS ARE AVID LISTENERS

Leaders often love to talk. They enjoy listening to their own great pearls of wisdom and insight. Sometimes they even begin to believe their own press reports. And as they gain more authority, they have less reason to listen to subordinates. Have you ever noticed that there is much more horizontal communication in an organization than vertical? Coworkers are always talking about everything, but the communication between those coworkers and their superiors is much less frequent and much more formal. Leaders must figure out ways to tap into that underground flow of information. They must keep current on the undercurrents.

The more people you lead, the more you must listen. Effective leadership has more to do with listening than with talking. Leaders, by their very nature, tend to be removed from the front lines of battle in the organization. Therefore, they must listen to those who are in the trenches and rely on that information to make wise decisions. Yet the pressures of leadership work against that process at every turn.

Here are some of the reasons why it is hard for leaders to listen to everyone in the organization:

Too little time. The more people you lead, the less time you have for each person. (And, of course, the more tasks each of them expects you to accomplish!)

Too many people. There are literally dozens of leaders in our organization

with whom I should have an intimate relationship, including the top leaders in the home office, the leaders of our field offices in North America, our
international directors, and the sixty-plus leaders of our projects around the
world. There are just too many of them, but they can each get individually
frustrated with me if I don't take the time or build the systems whereby they
can communicate with me.

Pressure. Leaders usually find themselves under a constant sense of pressure from more deadlines and responsibilities than they can handle well. The
image of a soldier in battle comes to mind: Here I stand in the trenches, with
bullets flying, planes buzzing overhead, and tanks rolling in our direction. My
radio is crackling with news from many fronts. Then along comes one of my
people who wants a quiet, long talk about his or her concerns. The intense
pressures of leadership sometimes make it very difficult to listen attentively,
which brings us back to chapter 2 and making time for people.

Distance. In some cases the sheer problem of physical distance
between the leader and his or her followers makes it tough to stay in close
contact. I have the challenge of many of our top leaders living five thousand miles away from me.

Too much knowledge. Leaders sometimes know so much that they find
it hard to listen to someone rehearsing stories, facts, or anecdotes that the
leader has already heard dozens of times.

Pride. This comes on the heels of the knowledge problem. Sometimes
we simply think we know too much. We get to the place where we don't
think we can learn from others. The admonition of Scripture should be
clear enough: "Be quick to listen [but] slow to speak" (James 1:19).

Communication overload. This problem was addressed in the paperwork versus peoplework discussion in chapter 2. The telecommunications
revolution is tightening the information noose around the neck of the
average leader. Leaders can become so saturated with communication that

they find their system shutting down from overload. With cell phones, notebook computers, faxes, e-mail, and BlackBerrys, you can run but you can't hide from communication overload.

Nothing stops the progress of an organization more quickly than leaders failing to listen. Like hardening of the arteries, restricted communication will destroy a leader's credibility. Followers want to communicate to their leaders. If you fail to listen to them, their very effectiveness and job satisfaction will be in jeopardy. At the end of this chapter, I will give tips on how I have overcome these obstacles in my leadership.

The Price of Leadership Isolation

Here are several real-life, anonymous accounts from wounded people who lost respect for leaders who didn't bother to listen. First, a young woman hurt by a leader who constantly cut her off:

> Our leader was a very "choleric" person. We were hurt by him many times. We expected he would wait and give us answers to our serious questions about our work. Many times he walked off in midsentence, having heard nothing. This happened to women more than men.

Then, there's the account of a youth director in a church, who was called to the carpet with no warning. He was caught in what I call "the ambush":

> While attending college I accepted a youth director's position at a local church. I dedicated approximately twenty to thirty hours a week working with junior and senior highers. After serving there for two years I was called into an elders meeting. One of the elders, who had three children in my ministry, took out a list of all the things I had done wrong in the

past two years. Most of what they said was true, for I was brand new in this work and made lots of mistakes. The next thing I knew, the elders were calling for my resignation in the heated emotions of the meeting. It came as a complete surprise. What did I learn? First, I cannot think of one instance in those two years that any of the elders or the pastor shepherded me in my ministry. Second, I had no idea nor warning that I was doing anything wrong. Finally, the leaders and staff had no significant relationships. Nobody could trust them.

And here is a letter from a frustrated follower stationed overseas, who found himself stuck with a leader who had no interest in listening:

Our team was voting on an issue. The majority of the members were in favor of the action, but the team leader was against it. As the votes were cast and didn't go his way, he gave a new explanation of the issue. We took another vote, with the same results. But he wouldn't give in until we voted six more times, always with the same results. It was a frustrating experience!

Certainly, if followers have a bill of rights, the right to be heard by their leader must be article one. I believe in strong leadership, but also in a strong leader who listens. Assuming that the group in that last example had a democratic process of decision making, the leader should have been in touch with the people enough to know where the decision was going. The incident just shows how out of touch he was with his followers.

COMMUNICATE THE BIG PICTURE WITH PASSION

Communication is especially important in the larger issues of corporate life. I encourage leaders to spell out their purposes, key goals, and core values, and to proclaim them from the rooftops. In fact, declaring the purpose and core values of an organization is one of the essential jobs of a leader. The staff who have been around a long time need to be reminded, and the new recruits need to be folded in to the corporate vision.

Here is a recent example from an organization that clearly communicates to newcomers exactly what it stands for. The organization is called CRM: Empowering Leaders, is led by Dr. Sam Metcalf, and is based in Fullerton, California.

The Expectations and Privileges of CRM Staff

As a staff person with CRM, it is fair for me to expect the following from those whom I follow throughout the organization. I can expect:

To know those who lead me and what they believe.

If I follow you, will I know who you are? What you are like? Are you authentic, honest, and will you deal with me with integrity?

To have leaders who will explain to me their vision.

What do you see for me? What's the future and where do I fit? Do you care about my future? Will you have a place for me or will you simply use me?

TO NEVER BE LEFT IN ISOLATION.

Are you there for me? Do you love me? Will you love me? Do you care about my cares, my concerns, my needs?

TO BE HEARD.

To whom will you listen? Will I be heard, taken seriously, and appreciated?

To be trusted.

Can I take initiative without fear? Will my creativity be rewarded and encouraged? Will I be respected?

To be provided a context for growth.

Will I be encouraged to be a lifelong learner? Will my gifts be increasingly identified and expressed? Can I live in a context where God's power can be freely manifested in my life? Will I be developed?

To be held accountable.

Will I be held accountable for personal godliness and holiness in all aspects of life and ministry? Will I be fairly evaluated for the performance of my responsibilities? Will I be lovingly held to God's best for my life?

To be the object of grace.

Will I be forgiven, even in the face of shortcomings, inadequacies, and failure? Will I have the freedom to be whom God has made me? Will I be led with kindness?

Another example of positive communication comes from one of the most successful companies in America, one that has truly placed God first in its business. Several months ago I had the opportunity to visit the national headquarters of the ServiceMaster Company. No one at ServiceMaster would ever be foggy about what the chief goals and vision of that organization are. It is literally plastered on the walls of their corporate offices.

Anyone considering becoming a partner with the ServiceMaster family, which is what they call employees, is expected to be committed to the company's corporate values:

ServiceMaster

We are in the business of serving others. This requires all of us to have an unending pursuit of excellence as we bring the benefit of our extraordinary service to our customers. This way of doing business can be best expressed by our four objectives. They are:

- ➤ To honor God in all that we do.
- ➤ To help people develop.
- ➤ To pursue excellence.
- ➤ To grow profitably.

THE NUTS AND BOLTS OF CLEAR COMMUNICATION

Clearing up chaotic communication in an organization is not easy. If you are building a new group from scratch, it is much easier. Whether you are starting over or are trying to be more faithful in clearing up cloudy communications, there are four basic areas where your followers need to be clear:

The vision and values of the group. Every group needs a clear mission statement indicating the strategic purpose of the organization. This mission statement is a clear declaration of vision. In addition to the mission/purpose statement, there should be an agreed upon set of clearly defined goals and objectives. This organizational blueprint needs to be communicated clearly, and updated as often as the nature of your work changes. (We'll take a closer look at the whole area of corporate values and culture in the next chapter, and a closer look at corporate vision in chapter 10.)

The chain of command. This may sound harsh in a world of flat organizations and decentralization, but it's not. It has to do with simply being clear on who is responsible for what. It is as important in a team-based group as in a traditional hierarchy. If your people have questions or problems, do they know who handles what in your organization? If they have a serious complaint, is there a clear path for their issues to rise to the top? When you have a project to assign within the group, do you know whose job it should be? If there is a major problem, do you know who is in charge of that area? These are all chain-of-command issues. Chain of command is simply the orderly division of responsibilities within an organization—making sure everyone knows who is responsible for what. If everyone is in charge, no one is in charge. Chain of command clarifies the questions of *who reports to whom, who supervises whom, and who is in charge of what.*

Organizational charts. We looked at some organizational charts in previous chapters. Organizational charts are an important part of clear communication. The idea of an organizational chart is not really new. Moses had a very detailed one. Does your group have an organizational chart? It is helpful for everyone in an organization to know where he or she fits. The "org chart" is a people map, outlining the relationships within the organization. It shows the lines of authority and responsibility. It enables everyone to visualize the chain of command.

Organizational charts help leadership see, in a quick, visual overview, just how the work of the company is organized. The charts also help the members of the organization know where they fit and where to go in the organization for help, resources, permissions, clearances, complaints, and grievances. They are also very helpful in explaining the corporate culture to the new members of your group. Organizational charts show the full scope of relationships in organizational life. Since those relationships change often, the charts should change as often as necessary. They should be simple, and they should be flexible, but most of all, they should simply be.

Job descriptions/position descriptions. Do your people have job descriptions? There are a thousand ways to write job descriptions, some quite complex and others very simple. I like job descriptions that lean toward simplicity. In our company we have moved to position descriptions that show what the basic responsibilities of a job entail. They need to be flexible and should outline three basic ingredients of any position: (1) primary responsibilities in the organization, (2) key activities and tasks performed to fulfill those responsibilities, and (3) reporting structure. With a clear job description, there can be no confusion between the leader and the follower about what that person is supposed to be doing. And it becomes the primary tool for evaluating effectiveness in an annual review system.

FINAL THOUGHTS

How do you know if your organization has communication chaos? Ask yourself how many of these symptoms are present:

1. Chaos and confusion about the group's direction.
2. Arguments or disagreements about priorities.
3. Duplication of effort.
4. Waste of resources through jobs that get canceled midstream.
5. Conflicts among departments.
6. Poor morale.
7. Poor productivity.
8. Idleness of resources.
9. Job insecurity.

There are no little people in your organization. Years ago, Francis Schaeffer wrote a significant book titled *No Little People.* He argued that in God's view there are no little people and no little places. All have equal value no matter where they are found and what they do. I think the same principle should be practiced by every Christian leader in their attitudes about the far-flung corners of their organizations. Everyone is important. Everyone has a right and a need to know what is going on in the organization—the big news as well as the little details. The more people are informed, the more they feel a part of the whole organization and the less chance there is for misunderstanding.

How do you feel if others know something you don't know? Have you ever learned significant news about your own organization from an outsider? Someone outside of leadership gave you the scoop on some juicy insider news. How does that make you feel? Insignificant? Hurt? Forgotten? Keep the troops informed. Have a passion to communicate, communicate, communicate. One really cannot overcommunicate. Listen to the advice of Max De Pree from *Leadership Is an Art*: "The right to know is basic. Moreover, it is better to err on the side of sharing too much information than risk leaving someone in the dark. Information is power, but it is pointless power if hoarded. Power must be shared for an organization or a relationship to work" (104–5).

How to avoid fossilization. As you looked at the chart on life cycles and communication at the beginning of this chapter, you may have thought, *I don't want us to become fossilized in the formal rituals of bureaucracy.* Here are a few tips to keep your organization lively as you commit more to written communication:

➤ Have regular press conferences with your people. Let them hear your heart. Allow them to ask you tough questions.

➤ Keep memos brief.

➤ Include one-page summaries on the top of lengthy reports.

➤ Use faxes and e-mail to keep communication fresh and up to the minute.

➤ Produce a concise written statement of vision and objectives that can be distributed throughout your organization.

➤ Have stand-up meetings to avoid lengthy discussions. Read *Death by Meeting* by Patrick Lencioni to learn how to do meetings right.

➤ Develop an in-house newsletter for weekly communication to the insiders.

➤ As the leader, cast the vision to insiders as much as you do to outsiders.

How to keep in touch with your people. After fifteen years as president and CEO of WorldVenture, I discovered as I looked back that the people I know the best are the ones whose homes I've visited or who have visited mine. That should be a no-brainer! There is no substitute for face time. We have to build personal relationships with our coworkers. Here is a summary of principles discussed and suggested in this chapter to help you avoid communication chaos:

➤ Have face time with your leaders.

➤ Play and pray with those you lead.

➤ Schedule regular off-site meetings for team development that include play as well as work.

➤ Make internal communications a top priority of your job.

➤ Keep your followers informed as to what you expect of them.

➤ Find ways to articulate and communicate vision and values.

➤ Make sure that formal communication systems are in place.

➤ Avoid the great surprise. Don't ambush people who are not doing their jobs well. Be honest.

➤ MbWA: Manage by Wandering Around. Get out of your office, but be sensitive to others achieving *their* goals/don't interrupt another's work flow.

➤ Find ways to tap into the underground within your organization. Have informants.

➤ Practice HOT communication: Honest, Open, and Transparent. Nothing happens until people talk.

QUICK TIPS FOR LEADERS ON THE GO

COMMUNICATION CHAOS

Singing from the Same Page in the Hymnal

Big Idea: Communication systems are the arteries in an organization. Without good blood flow, an organization can become sick. Leaders must make communication a vital aspect of every day, and that communication must focus in four directions: inward, outward, upward, and downward. Both employees and customers or constituents should be informed of the direction of leadership. As should both those who work below us as well as those who work above us. We never communicate enough, and we usually communicate way less than we think we do. It is a rare organization that has been found guilty of over-communicating.

> ➤ *Never assume that anyone knows anything.* Most of us live in the dark about what is really going on in the organizations we are a part of. We should just assume that no one is informed and take the necessary time to tell them. Repeat, repeat, repeat.

> ➤ *The bigger the group, the more attention that must be given to communication.* The bigger organizations get, the more formal communication must become. Startups are usually small enough for verbal communication to get the

job done. But as offices are added and the walls go higher, formal communication becomes more critical than ever but is often ignored.

➤ *When left in the dark, people tend to dream up wild rumors.* This is where human nature always shows its dark side. People tend to think the worst of each other, instead of the best. Rumors destroy morale, and are best grown in the fertile soil of a communication-less organization. It is the job of effective leaders to build communication bridges throughout their organization and make sure that people are talking to each other.

➤ *Communication must be the passionate obsession of effective leadership.* Leaders love to talk about vision, but they often fall short of selling it. The higher you go in an organization, the more you must give yourself to telling and selling the vision to those inside and out.

MISSING THE CLUES OF CORPORATE CULTURE

8

The Unseen Killer of Many Leaders

> ➤ Corporate culture is "the way we do things around here."
> ➤ Never underestimate the mighty power of your organization's culture.
> ➤ Cultivating and changing the culture should be one of leadership's top priorities.
> ➤ Learn to respect values different from your own.

Get rid of those donuts and bring out the bran muffins!" I told my secretary after my first experience at a staff social event. "Haven't these people discovered the low-fat revolution?"

"Take it easy, Hans. This is the Midwest, not California," she warned me.

Here was another example of corporate culture staring me in the face as I was getting adjusted to working in a new organizational setting in a new part of the country. After having spent quite a bit of our married lives in California, it was a shock to get used to life in the Midwest. We love the people of Chicago, but they do eat differently than Californians!

> ## CORPORATE CULTURE
>
> An organization's corporate culture is the way insiders behave based on the values and group traditions they hold.

I have been intrigued to observe the concept of corporate culture during the past fifteen years, and have made it a hobby to observe the cultures of organizations I come in contact with. Here are a few living illustrations of what corporate culture is all about:

The boss calls in one of his new employees after several weeks on the job and says the following, "This corporation prides itself on being a friendly place to work, Matthews, and from now on, we want you to be a heck of a lot friendlier."

A new woman working in a dentist's office is pulled aside by another employee and is reprimanded by her after several weeks on the job: "We dance the waltz around here. If you dance the polka, you won't make it."

A father, speaking to his son with pearls of wisdom as he is about to enter the marketplace after graduation from college shares with him the first rule of survival in a new job: "Find out how they keep score and score."

I define corporate culture very simply as "the way we do things around here." Or to make the definition a bit more formal: "An organization's corporate culture is the way insiders behave based on the values and group traditions they hold."

Take this quiz to see if you have ever bumped into corporate culture. Answer yes or no to the following questions:

1. Are you a Mac or a PC fanatic?
2. Does your personality change when you go to see your in-laws? Does your spouse's?
3. Have you felt the anxiety and surprise of moving into a new job?
4. Did you make any adjustments in your life when you got married?
5. Have you tried to reform or "reprogram" your spouse?
6. Have you experienced the changed dynamics and pressure of having to adjust to a new boss?
7. Do you find more esprit de corps and compatibility with certain kinds of people?
8. Have you ever felt you just don't fit with the group you work with?
9. Have you had serious disagreements with other committed Christians who believe in the same Bible you do?
10. Can you separate your theology from methodology?
11. Do you ever feel that your coworkers just don't share your values?
12. Are you devoted to a particular airline? To a certain line of automobile?
13. Are there certain groups or organizations you would not work for at any price?
14. If you were in charge, would you change your organization significantly?

If you answered yes to most of those questions, you have run into corporate culture. Organizational culture is like the glue in plywood—you are not totally aware of it until you try to take it apart!

I look at corporate culture the same way I look at human faces and personalities. Isn't it amazing that no two faces are exactly alike? With billions of people on earth, God in his infinite creativity has designed every one of us with a different face, voice, fingerprint, and personality. Organizations are the same way. Each one has a totally unique and distinct personality. Its culture is built upon the values and belief systems that percolate up from the core of its leadership like molten lava bubbling out of a volcano.

Just what is organizational culture? And what, if anything, does it have to do with leadership? The term *culture* was for many years the domain of the anthropologist and sociologist. But today it has become a buzzword in leadership and management circles. Anyone who has an interest in leadership or management will run into the concept of corporate culture on a regular basis. It is discussed broadly in a wide range of applications and is increasingly recognized as one of the fundamental building blocks of organizational life.

Corporate culture is a powerful force. It can at times be so strong that people develop a religious attitude toward their company, so devoted they are to its culture.

WHERE CORPORATE CULTURE SHOWS UP

If you're married, you felt a strong dose of corporate culture when you realized that your spouse's family was not like your own. I vividly remember the clash of cultures when Donna and I got married. My private, closed German upbringing thrown into her warm open family culture created a lot of sparks in the early years. Each family, like each organization, has its own values that create a unique set of behavioral patterns. Through the years we blended the two families and created our own unique Finzel culture.

While I was in graduate school in Dallas, I worked for several different companies over a short span of time. I recall the culture shock as I moved from one job to the next. First I worked the night shift at a Fleischmann's margarine factory. That was my first exposure to dyed-in-the-wool union people. What a tight culture! I was nonunion, and they kept reminding me of it. That job lasted two weeks.

I then took a job in sales for a security firm, where I was thrown into a fellowship of off-duty policemen. What a culture the law enforcement crowd is! They were worlds away from the Fleischmann's group. About a year later I went to work in the construction and remodeling industry in north Dallas, fixing up grand old homes that were being revived. Again I found a distinct new subculture of people in professional painters and carpenters.

WHERE CULTURE CROPS UP

➤ A new marriage
➤ A new church
➤ A new city
➤ A new job
➤ A new pastor
➤ A new boss
➤ A new generation
➤ Conflict
➤ Preferences
➤ Tastes
➤ Lifestyles

If you've moved from one organization to another, you felt corporate culture as you learned a new set of unwritten rules. When you walk into a new organization for the first time, you can feel the culture much more than an insider can. It has been observed that you cannot understand your own culture until you have traveled to another. The first time you visit another country for a few weeks, you begin to realize that the whole world does not think or act as North Americans do. And when you step off the plane back home, you see your own culture as never before. You get a small glimpse of what foreigners see when they first land on our shores.

Newcomers to organizations have the same feeling when they step "on the shore" of a new group. They feel that they have to learn "how to do things around here," and if they don't, fellow workers will let them know. Ralph Kidman writes:

> The organization itself has an invisible quality—a certain style, a character, a way of doing things—that may be more powerful than the dictates of any one person or any formally documented system. To understand the essence or soul of the organization requires that we travel below the charts, rulebooks, machines, and buildings into the underground world of corporate cultures. (*Beyond the Quick Fix,* 92)

ORGANIZATIONAL CULTURE AND LEADERSHIP

Just what is culture? It's a fuzzy term that means different things to different people. William B. Renner of the Aluminum Company of America highlights the dilemma of defining culture:

> Culture is different things to different people. For some, it's family or religion. It's opera or Shakespeare, a few clay pots at a Roman dig. Every textbook offers a definition, but I like a simple one: culture is the shared values and behavior that knit a community together. It's the rules of the game; the unseen meaning between the lines in the rule book that assures unity. All organizations have a culture of their own (ibid., 92).

Merriam-Webster's Collegiate Dictionary defines culture as: "the integrated pattern of human knowledge, belief, and behavior that depends upon the capacity for learning and transmitting knowledge to succeeding generations; the customary beliefs, social forms, and material traits of a racial, religious, or social group."

Traditionally, culture has been defined simply as the unique *customs, values,* and *artifacts* of a people. Today there is a growing consensus that organizations have distinct cultures as well, the same distinct customs, values, and artifacts that we usually think of societies possessing. It is also a growing conviction in management circles that those cultures need to be understood, nurtured, and managed. If you miss the culture clues as a leader, you may be in for some tough times.

Intel and Avis are often cited as examples of companies that are successful because they devote much of their energies to the promotion and cultivation of corporate culture. They put much of their energy into managing employees' behavior through creating a strong culture.

In 1982 Thomas Peters and Robert Waterman wrote an immensely popular book, *In Search of Excellence: Lessons from America's Best-Run Companies,* in which they showed the benefits and characteristics of the strong corporate cultures of America's best-run organizations. Peters and Waterman brought to focus a *realization that strong cultures contribute to organizational success when the culture supports the mission, goals, and strategy of the organization.*

The pursuit of excellence is certainly something that anyone involved in leading a Christian organization ought to be about. The Bible compels us to do whatever we do to the glory of God: "So whether you eat or drink or whatever you do, do it all for the glory of God" (1 Cor. 10:31). "And whatever you do, whether in word or deed, do it all in the name of the Lord Jesus, giving thanks to God the Father through him" (Col. 3:17). A few verses later, Paul states, "Whatever you do, work at it with all your heart, as working for the Lord, not for men, since you know that you will receive an inheritance from the Lord as a reward. It is the Lord Christ you are serving" (vv. 23–24).

THE HUMAN SIDE OF CHRISTIAN ORGANIZATIONS

My wife, Donna, works for an exciting nutritional company that is part of the growing wellness industry. Twice a year I go to their national conventions where thousands of happy people get inspired and work at improving themselves. We have been going to these meetings for years, and I love them! It is so much fun to be with a group of people filled with such passion and positive direction. When I contrast her meetings with the less-than-inspiring Christian conventions I have attended in the past, it is a sad realization. As we compare notes, I am amazed that there is often a more supportive community and more care for improving people in her company than in many churches.

For many Christians it is more fulfilling and enjoyable to work in well-run secular organizations than in the poorly organized, stressful environments of many Christian organizations. To put it even more simply, it is often a whole lot more fun to work in the world than in the church. Why? Because the church is frequently behind on understanding basic principles of how humans work well together. It is often a leadership problem. Jesus knew that nonbelievers often make wiser leaders than the sons of the kingdom: The master commended the dishonest manager because he had acted shrewdly. For the people of this world are more shrewd in dealing with their own kind than are the people of light (Luke 16:8).

It was the steward's astuteness, not his morality that was commended. One commentator rewrites the passage like this: "The children of this world look further ahead, in dealing with their own generation, than the children of light" (Morris, 248). Anyone who has worked in a Christian organization for very long knows that each Christian group has its own way of doing things. Whether secular or sacred, organizations have cultures and each is unique. And these ways of doing things are passed down from founders to their heirs, generation after generation.

SO HOW DO WE FIND OUR CORPORATE CULTURE?

The obvious question at this point is: How do I know what our organization's culture is? One way to answer this question is to take some time to sit down with your leadership group and describe your corporate culture. I suggest using two categories by making a distinction between your organization's values and beliefs: call values "preferences" and beliefs, "moral absolutes."

CONTRASTING VALUES AND BELIEFS IN CORPORATE CULTURE

Values	Beliefs
Preferences	Moral absolutes
Tastes	Black and white
Regional and cultural	Ethical issues
Methodology, not theology	Right and wrong values

Here are some samples of values (preferences) and beliefs (moral absolutes). As you read the list, answer these questions: Which of these values or beliefs would I fight over? Which of these would I quit my job over? Which are nonnegotiable? Which do I disagree with? Put a plus in the margin by the values and beliefs that you agree with. Put a minus by the ones that you are neutral on, and strike out the ones you strongly oppose. When you're done, ask yourself this question: *How many of my colleagues would answer as I have?*

VALUES OR PREFERENCES

➤ We will use the latest technology to do our work.

➤ More technology is better than less.

➤ Time is more valuable than money.

➤ The reduction of paperwork is important.

➤ We won't do it if it's not quality.

➤ Anything important will be written in a report.

➤ Speed is of the essence.

➤ Precision is of the essence.

➤ Better to do it right than to fail because it was not perfect.

➤ Our people must learn the languages in the countries or regions where we work.

➤ We will submit to the cultures of the other lands or regions in which we work.

BELIEFS OR MORAL ABSOLUTES

➤ We will have open, honest relationships and ask forgiveness if we wrong another worker in our organization.

➤ Theft will not be tolerated among our people.

➤ My children come before my work.

➤ Lying has no place between our workers.

➤ We will not hold on to bitterness.

➤ We cannot tolerate immorality among our workers.

➤ Planting new churches is the best way to fulfill the Great Commission.

➤ We must show compassion to the poor and suffering.

➤ The Bible is God's inerrant, inspired revelation to mankind.

➤ Our workers must be ethnically diverse.

If you compare your responses to that list with a colleague's, you may find you even disagree about which list a particular item should be on. What one person thinks is a value another may view as a belief, an absolute. I know Mac owners who are convinced that it's morally responsible to be loyal to Apple! To some people the world is black-and-white, and everything is a moral issue. Such people are hard to work with and hard to work for. They are inflexible and tend to think their way is the only way.

> ## CORPORATE VALUE STATEMENTS ARE:
>
> ➤ Like Glue—They help leaders hold an organization together.
> ➤ Like a Magnet—They attract newcomers as members, employees, customers, or donors.
> ➤ Like a Ruler—By which a leader can measure how his or her group is doing.

Understanding the difference between values and beliefs has been very liberating for me. I learned to give up the right to be right when it is not a moral or ethical issue. Some issues simply are not worth fighting over. Many times we have to respect the rights of others to have a different set of values than ours.

As a leader, spend some time alone and really think about your own values and beliefs. Then work with your leadership team and list the values and beliefs your whole team believes in. This list will become the unmitigated glue that holds your team together like layers in a sheet of plywood.

Secular companies know this principle well. Donna and I love shopping at Whole Foods Market. On a wall near the registers are the company's value statements. Go to its Web site and read the meaty details they unpack as they describe each of these values. They are the best corporate value statements I've seen, and I believe Whole Foods holds true to them, because we shop there and see those values in action.

WHOLE FOODS MARKET'S CORE VALUES
1. Selling the Highest Quality Natural and Organic Products Available
2. Satisfying and Delighting Our Customers
3. Supporting Team Member Excellence and Happiness
4. Creating Wealth Through Profits & Growth
5. Caring About Our Communities & Our Environment

One of the most successful mail order companies in America is Lands' End, based in Wisconsin. These premier direct-mail merchants have boiled down their culture into four clearly articulated corporate values. These four pillars of the company determine daily actions in organizational life:

LANDS' END
1. Make your merchandise as good as you can.
2. Always, always price it fairly.
3. Make it a snap to shop for, twenty-four hours a day.
4. Guarantee it, period.

Sun Valley Waterbeds, based on the West Coast, has become one of America's top providers of a good night's sleep. The company knows what it is after and has articulated it well in its communications, first with its employees and then to its customers:

SUN VALLEY WATERBEDS
"Our Precepts"
1. We believe that we sincerely provide a better night's sleep.
2. We believe our products are of a proven high quality at a fair price, representing the best possible value.

3. We believe in serving customers in such a manner as to earn their continuing respect, confidence, trust, and support, both before and after the sale.

4. We believe we should treat our customers, dealers, suppliers, and employees with human dignity and integrity, observing the highest moral and ethical standards in all aspects of our business.

5. We believe the customer is always right.

6. We believe in being a good corporate citizen by contributing to the economic and social well-being of every community in which we operate.

7. We believe in being the most respected company in the industry.

Finally, here is an example from a local church that has taken the same principle and clearly articulated its core values in a simple-to-remember format. Rick Warren, the highly effective pastor of Saddleback Church in Lake Forest, California, and author of *The Purpose-Driven Life*, spells out to his church and to the public at large the values that guide the church:

THE SADDLEBACK STRATEGY

1. Simple structure: We emphasize relationships.

2. Acceptance: We offer friendliness and openness.

3. Defined purpose: We exist for four distinct reasons—to celebrate God's presence, communicate His Word, educate His people, and demonstrate His love.

4. Defined target: To respond to the hurts, needs, and interests of our community.

5. Lay ministry: Our church runs by lay ministries.

6. Encouraging preaching: Our preaching emphasizes personal, practical solutions from God's Word for life's common problems.

7. Build up before building out: We build people before buildings.

8. Advertising: We do so to share our church with the community.

9. Contemporary worship: A style that is culturally relevant.

10. Keep on growing: Because everybody needs what Christ offers.

THE VALUE OF UNDERSTANDING CORPORATE CULTURE

"Culture audits" are valuable for Christian organizations for many reasons. They can help leaders understand the underlying dynamics that drive their organization. Beliefs and values that are circulating deep beneath the surface can be identified, discussed, and evaluated. Here are some ways your organization can benefit from understanding its own corporate culture:

You can better evaluate your organization's representation of Christian values and beliefs. For the Christian organization, whether a mission agency, a parachurch group, a church, or a church-related group, there should be distinctions that make it different from secular institutions in the way it operates. The Christian should uphold viewpoints rooted in biblical Christianity that differ noticeably from a secular worldview. In reality, what an organization espouses as its Christian values and beliefs often differs dramatically from its actual practices. For example, the group can say that it values family life but then demand so much from its leaders that their families are ruined in the process. Any Christian organization must ask itself if it is truly practicing what it upholds as the necessary standards for Christian ministry.

You can evaluate your organizational effectiveness. Many writers in the field of organizational culture point to the issue of group effectiveness as one of the most far-reaching benefits of understanding corporate culture. The culture of an organization can work for or against the goals of the group. Major problems can arise in a group that has developed values or beliefs in conflict with the actual mission of the group. As an example, I know of a ministry with the goal to be innovative and contemporary in evangelizing America's youth culture. Yet the organization is burdened with a stifling paper bureaucracy that lives in the past and is slow to change. It has a future-oriented ministry purpose, tied to a culture rooted in tradition looking at the past.

Groups shouldn't take on goals that are incompatible with the organization's underlying assumptions. To understand the culture of the organization is to know what the organization is good at doing and what it should avoid.

You'll have a better understanding of division and strife. There are actually different subcultures within any organization. At times two subcultures can become so incompatible that they split, an event that often happens in local church settings. I have witnessed more than a few churches fighting over forms of worship and music, with different subcultures each believing that their way is the right way.

A large Christian organization that ministers to children recently had a major rift that came to the surface after several years of tension. A large subculture within the organization, which included some of the top leadership, left to begin a new work with identical goals. The members of the group that departed had become so uncomfortable in the "host culture," that they felt their only option was disassociation.

Basic assumptions and beliefs in the two subcultures had become incompatible.

A culture audit can bring to the surface conflicts burrowed deep within the organization that are stifling all possibilities for effectiveness.

Leaders who understand their own values and can articulate them well to their organization have proven to show superior performance in their roles. In *The Leadership Challenge,* James Kouzes and Barry Posner list six significant payoffs for both managers and their organizations when the leaders were able to articulate a unified, distinct organizational culture. Understanding your organization's culture:

1. fosters strong feelings of personal effectiveness;
2. promotes high levels of company loyalty;
3. facilitates consensus about key organizational goals;
4. encourages ethical behavior;
5. reduces levels of job stress and tension;
6. promotes strong norms about working hard and caring.
—Kouzes and Posner, *The Leadership Challenge*

You'll have increased leadership compatibility. In the case just described, one subculture felt incompatible with another. In some situations a leader is incompatible with the culture of the group. This is often the case when a search committee recruits a new leader without doing the necessary culture homework. The basic assumptions of the prospective new leader should be compared with the basic assumptions of the organization for cultural compatibility. Such a comparison can easily be done during the recruitment stage. The search committee should look at how the potential pastor or leader looks at various issues that the host group holds dear. Unfortunately, usually much more emphasis is placed on infatuation and subjective feelings than on deep discussion about values and beliefs.

Leaders must be a good cultural fit for the organization in order to enjoy a long tenure of effective service. I recently watched three such recruitment efforts go up in smoke. An organization based in Georgia recruited a new leader from the West who seemed pleasant on the outside. They fell in love with him during a quick weekend interview. The problem came when this new executive alienated everyone within a few short months because of his general negative attitude toward the "ways of the South." It was a cultural mismatch and the person soon moved his family back to California.

In another example, a strong leader was recruited for a church that held plurality of leadership as its basic approach to management. The leader felt he was in charge, but the group of leaders who recruited him felt he would be only one among equals, and that all decisions would be made in the group, by consensus. Needless to say, conflicts soon arose and the pastor soon left.

And finally, a church recruited a senior pastor who was a mismatch basically because his career experience was in a blue-collar background and had led only blue-collar congregations. The new church was a high-tech urban church that was initially wowed by his preaching but soon found that nothing he said was connecting with them. It did not work out either.

You'll have accountability of leadership's behavior. Christian leaders should act differently than those in the secular world. They should treat their workers differently, they should view their mission in a different light, and they should be driven by different motivations. Since the leader is the keeper of the culture, it falls on his or her shoulders to cultivate a culture that is distinctly Christian. The values and beliefs that a leader holds usually become the assumptions of the followers. That puts a great deal of responsibility on the shoulders of leadership.

Christian leaders should strive to live a model of servant leadership that is distinct from the secular corporate executive in basic areas. A mission CEO recently resigned overnight to take a new position with another organization. The shock of his resignation was damaging to the organization, because it had made so many changes in ministry strategy at his request. After only a few years in the CEO position, and after making many deep changes in the mission, the leader simply walked away with no warning. When asked by the chairman of the board why he did not share his desire to move on or discuss the move with anyone, the former CEO replied, "Well, that's the way they do it in the corporate world; it's all very secret." In the work of the church, things ought to be different.

You'll enjoy better recruitment and placement of personnel. Equally as important as the fit of the leader with the organizational culture is the fit of the followers. When an organization is recruiting staff, it must be careful to choose people who are culturally compatible and it must be honest with potential recruits about the corporate culture they are being asked to join.

When I am recruiting for our organization, I know exactly what we value and stand for. The more I can communicate that clearly, the more potential recruits will get an honest appraisal of what it would be like to work for us. Too many people are promised one thing only to discover an entirely different world when they go to work on their first day.

Your staff will be better trained. I can think of no better way to orient new staff to your group than to take them point by point through your list of values and beliefs. By doing so, you are (a) teaching them what you believe, (b) explaining to them why you emphasize what you emphasize, and (c) indoctrinating them into the very soul of the organization.

You'll more effectively discern career choices. On the other side of recruitment is discernment in regard to your career. When you're looking for a group to join or an organization to work for, it is imperative that the person conducting the search investigate the basic cultural values of the group and compare those with his or her own. Figure out where they stand before you throw your hat in the ring with them.

There are as many types of organizations, with vastly different values and beliefs, as there are people. Instead of walking into a situation that is a poor cultural fit, it would be better for the person doing the seeking to try to work with a group that, as closely as possible, shares his or her values and beliefs.

You can more intelligently decide on mergers, acquisitions, or joint efforts. I recently watched two organizations here in Colorado merge, and within six months they had gone out of business. They were both weak and struggling and thought that the merger would solve all their woes. Fundamentally, there was a strong cultural mismatch that was never explored or acknowledged. There are times when Christian groups, like secular corporations, find it helpful to merge, acquire, or work jointly with other groups. In all of these situations it is helpful to ask questions about cultural compatibility before the groups come together. One can anticipate problems that may arise—and they usually do—if one can see the difference in assumptions between the groups.

One company, for example, began to work with another that had strong differences in its views regarding time, resources, and relationships. Company A held that communication should be formal, through written memos and correspondence. Relationships were primarily official and communicated through clear lines of administrative channels, systems, and paperwork. Company B, in contrast, valued networking and informal, open lines of communication and did not use paper to communicate. If one person at company B needed to get a message to another, the telephone was the tool of choice, regardless of long-distance costs. At company A, no one used the phone to communicate.

As the two groups began to work together, company B angered the leaders at company A with their constant interrupting, "wasteful" phone calls, while company B was annoyed at the unresponsiveness at company A and ignored their "bureaucratic" flood of paperwork. To this day the two groups have not learned to communicate because of their radically different organizational cultures.

You'll have clearer vision of leadership and change. One of the core jobs of a leader is to be the "tender of the culture," the person who nurtures and develops the group's understanding of itself. The more he or she knows about the group's existing culture, the easier it will be to lead and to promote needed change.

TO FIT OR NOT TO FIT:
CULTURAL HARMONY AND DISSONANCE

All of the issues just explored have one thing in common: they deal with issues of cultural fit. Cultural fit can be viewed in terms of harmony and dissonance. Understanding the unique organizational culture of a group of people helps one understand who fits with that group and who does not. Whether dealing with followers or leaders, new employees or old, there are people who fit in organizations and others who don't.

At times the lack of fit is in the area of beliefs, where moral issues of right and wrong are at stake. Other times it is in the values area, in which one person feels strongly about doing things in a way that is not the common practice of the group.

These important issues of harmony and dissonance can be seen in the following Cultural Harmony illustration, which uses circles to represent different people and a big circle to represent the organization with its corporate culture.

Cultural Harmony

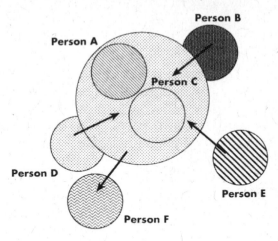

Think of the big circle as your organization with its unique culture. Person A is working for you, but doesn't really fit or feel at home. (More in a moment on what happens to people like him.) Persons B and E are unlike A and are on their way into the group from the outside. They are new employees/members who will either change to conform to the group or become like person A, not feeling at home. Persons C and D are ideal, for they completely share the values and beliefs of the group. You need a lot of Cs and Ds, but don't forget that the absence of some mavericks will eventually spell institutionalized boredom! Don't drive away all the Fs because they think differently.

The more a person buys into the corporate value and belief system of an organization, the more cultural harmony there will be between that person and the group. And conversely, the more differences there are, the more one finds dissonance within the group.

CULTURAL ADAPTATION:
WHO STAYS AND WHO LEAVES?

Dealing with these issues of cultural harmony and dissonance leads to the important issue of cultural adaptation. Not everyone within an organization has totally committed themselves to the organizational culture, the values and beliefs of the core group. Especially for newcomers, it may take months to uncover the core and learn what the people really believe. When there is dissonance within the group's beliefs and values, newcomers will either

1. adapt wholeheartedly and promote the culture enthusiastically;

2. adapt reluctantly and submit to the culture passively;

3. reject the culture and try to change it;

4. reject the culture and be a troublemaker, while remaining miserable;

5. reject the culture and leave;

6. reject the culture and make everyone miserable trying to change it.

Cultural fit issues are also applicable in Christian organizations. Though we may read the same Bible, we don't all believe the same way. As you may know, Christians differ dramatically in both beliefs and values and can best serve the church if they join with Christians who see things in roughly the same way they do. Through the centuries, many strains of Christians have emerged because of subtle differences. I believe God created different kinds of Christians to reach different kinds of people. Use the principle of "different strokes for different folks" and join a group you find culturally compatible.

FINAL THOUGHTS

HARNESS YOUR CORPORATE CULTURE

Write your perceived culture on paper. Have your leadership team individually list their values and beliefs. Use one page for each. After each has written them, share them among the team and compare them.

Compile, then integrate and simplify your group's list of corporate values and beliefs. Move from individual views to those the group as a whole holds most important. When you complete this process you will have a list of your organization's core values.

Develop a vision statement. Develop a statement that reflects where you envision going and growing as a group. Make sure all your top leaders are a part of writing this statement and that they believe in it 100 percent.

SIX REACTIONS TO CULTURE CONFLICT

Conformer
"I've just got to accept things the way they are."

Complainer
"I may have to work here, but I don't have to like it.

Innovator
"Let's change things around here!"

Ritualist
"Job? What job? I'm just going through the motions."

Retreatist
"I've got to get out of this situation ASAP!"

Rebel
"They can't make me conform—I'll show them!"

Communicate your culture clearly to insiders and outsiders. When the culture is identified and the mission clearly stated, preach it from the rooftops to both insiders and your constituents or customers.

Listen to win. Develop the ability to listen to others who don't agree with you.

Learn to like those who are different. The Bible teaches us to accept one another in love. Peter was rebuked for his bad attitude toward those who were unlike him. Learn to love and accept those who differ from you (see Acts 10:9–38).

Learn to separate methodology from theology. For those of you who are passionate about doctrine, draw your line in the sand where it counts, but don't make *value* differences *moral* issues. Hold to your theology passionately, but don't force your moral preferences on everyone else. There are many ways to interpret the Bible, and we need to learn to keep the plain things the main things.

QUICK TIPS FOR LEADERS ON THE GO

MISSING THE CLUES OF CORPORATE CULTURE
The Unseen Killer of Many Leaders

Big Idea: Every business, church, or company has its own culture. Companies are like families, no two of which behave exactly the same. Corporate "culture" is the way a company behaves based on the values and traditions its employees hold. Successful leaders learn how to harness the culture of their group for the common good.

➤ *Never underestimate the mighty power of your organization's culture.* It is impossible to initiate change in an organization without first understanding its culture.

➤ *Cultivating and changing culture should be one of leadership's top priorities.* Changing the culture in an organization takes a Herculean effort over many years, but it can be done. It is through those efforts that real lasting change takes root.

➤ *Learn to respect values different from your own.* Values are relative, beliefs are absolute. Learning the difference is an essential task for leaders as they learn to sift through their corporate culture. Sometimes we must learn to give up on the smaller issues so we can affect the larger ones.

SUCCESS WITHOUT SUCCESSORS

*Planning Your Departure
the Day You Start*

➤ Pride tightens the grip on leadership; humility relaxes
  and lets go.
➤ Finishing well is an important measure of success in
  leadership.
➤ Letting go of leadership is like sending your children
  away to college: It hurts, but has to be done.
➤ Mentoring is a nonnegotiable function of successful
  leadership.

There I was, right in the middle of trench warfare between the old guy
and his new successor. What a rude awakening to the terrors that
some leadership transitions take on.

Right out of graduate school I joined the staff of a large church in Southern California. The pastor who hired me was new himself, having just taken over for the former pastor who had been at the helm for twenty-six years. It's hard for anyone to follow such a long tenure of leadership, but what set this situation up for disaster was the decision of the church trustees to allow the former pastor to stay on the pastoral team for a two-year transition. The declining, graying congregation that had grown up with this pastor thought, *Since our leader has been so wonderful for so many years, who can possibly replace him and run our beloved institution?*

So the trustees and tenured pastor hatched a plan: though ill-fated, their intent was good. They decided to look for a new pastor, who, during his first year, would be mentored by the old pastor. The plan was that during the second year, the two would switch roles, with the older man becoming an assistant to the new man. After two years the old guy would ride off into the sunset and the church would boldly face the future in peace and harmony.

What's wrong with this picture? Nothing, in a perfect world. But it failed to take into account two major issues: pride of leadership and the depravity of man. Soon after the new, younger man (who, by the way, was in his fifties) arrived, he began to generate a following among the younger, more aggressive people in the church who wanted change. The older man, with the old guard, began to feel threatened. Soon the older pastor let it

> ## LEADERSHIP TRANSITIONS
>
> Of all the leadership transition mistakes, two occur most frequently:
>
> ➤ Leaders tend to stay too long in a position rather than not long enough.
> ➤ Leaders who stay too long do much more damage than those who don't stay long enough.
> —Lyle Schaller

be known that he was not pleased with the new direction taken by his new associate.

The shoe finally dropped during the final weeks of that hot August, and the older pastor resigned in protest of his successor's direction. Fast-forwarding to the ultimate outcome, the church developed a vicious division into two camps—the old versus the new—and the new pastor was voted out of the church. The church was left leaderless and deeply divided. Twenty-five years later, it still never recovered from the immaturity and damage of that failed leadership transition. Though the older pastor spent many fruitful years leading that church, he did not finish well, and he ruined his successor's chance for success.

In vivid contrast, as different as the midnight sky is to high noon, I found myself again in the middle of a major leadership transition a decade later. This one worked with textbook order. In this case, the older man—leader for twenty-two years—turned over the reins and walked away in gracious humility.

He handed those reins to me.

As I mentioned before, when I became president of WorldVenture, we were a fifty-year-old organization. I was a part of an amazingly organized leadership transition that endured the test of time. I look back fifteen years later and still have great admiration for the humility of the man who went before me. My predecessor, Warren Webster, finished well by focusing on the future even though he knew he would not be a part of it.

While I was in the process of being screened for appointment, I clearly recall a statement Warren made to me: "Success without a successor is fail-ure." He honestly believed this principle and lived it out by allowing a smooth and orderly transfer of power.

I remember asking him, "How can I ever fill your shoes?" He smiled and said, "I don't want you to. I am taking my shoes with me!

You need to be your own man." I saw Warren later. He was nearing eighty and suffered the terrible effects of Parkinson's disease. It is hard for him to talk, and he lives in a wheelchair. But he still encourages me and is one of my biggest fans. Warren's method is what I call a successful leadership transition.

How many leaders at that stage in life make things ugly by not leaving when they should, or by undermining the new leader? In contrast, Webster affirmed me, supported me, mentored me, and launched me into new role with great fanfare. And he knew my leadership style was as different from his as night is from day. It was obvious to him that our organization needed change, and he communicated this to the board of directors and senior staff. Upon his departure I told him, "I hope when it comes my turn to hand the reins to my successor that I will have half of the graciousness and humility that you have had."

THE ONGOING SUCCESSOR SEARCH

Success without a successor is failure. Who are the men and women you are grooming who may one day take your place? I keep a running list in my laptop of up-and-coming leaders who may someday be ready to pick up where I leave off. I look at them and think, *Yes, he could become director of this; she will be ready for this role in a few years.* In fact, sometimes as I speak to our younger staff, I look into their faces and think, *One of you will replace me someday!* That thought excites and motivates me to pave the way for them. They are not a threat but the ultimate continuation of my leadership beginnings. I recently implemented a president's intern program to have these young leaders shadow me for a year. One of them will someday replace me, so they might as well learn the challenges firsthand from me now.

Organizations live and die on their flow and acceptance of new leadership talent. As we saw in chapter 4 when considering corporate life cycles, the only way to guarantee that your group does not slide down the back side of the curve to institutionalization, calcification, and death is to constantly renew with the fresh blood of new leaders.

One of my priorities as a leader is mentoring our emerging leadership pool. I'm in my fifties, and they are in their twenties and early thirties. I will watch, help, and nurture them whenever I can. As often as possible, I ask myself, *Who are my men? Who are the people I am targeting and developing for leadership? Where are the women who will lead us?* This is not playing favorites, it is preparing for the future.

If we build it, will they come? Not necessarily. One thing I have become obsessed with in the past couple of years is studying emerging generations. If we want them to join our organizations or churches, we have to throw out the welcome mat in some unusual ways. In postmodern America, young people have changed more than many realize. Those born after 1975 don't want to be like baby boomers, but they do want us to mentor them. I have to allow our culture to change at WorldVenture again: to become less boomer and more emergent. If we don't change, they will not come.

Every one of the more than 650 people who work in our global organization warrants my attention as his or her leader. Because I cannot be close to everyone, I must work through the senior staff who surround me at our headquarters. I keep one eye trained on leading our present leaders and the other on the rising pool of new talent. The eye that is trained on new talent looks through the sight of a rifle, not a shotgun. I cannot develop everyone to lead at the highest levels, because many follow and few lead. Without showing favoritism, I focus on the few rising stars who seem to show greatest promise.

I watch these men and women and encourage their advancement

CHARACTERISTICS OF EMERGING GENERATIONS BORN AFTER 1975

➤ Long for a sense of belonging
➤ Value authenticity, transparency, and humility
➤ Emphasize praxis over dogma, deeds over creeds
➤ Function best with flat, fluid leadership structure
➤ Focus in their micro story (facebook.com and myspace.com), not one big macro story
➤ Admire kingdom thinkers—not empire builders
➤ Find meaning in ambiguity, paradox, metaphor, mystery, and artistic creativity
➤ Expect and demand meaningful engagement
➤ View the Bible as the story of God's redemptive purpose rather than the repository of propositional truth

through growing degrees of responsibility and levels of leadership. I listen to what others say about them—an informal but very effective way to get references! And, of course, I look for two important traits of successful leaders: how well they *get along with people* and how good they are at *accomplishing excellent work.* This is nothing more than the sound principle Jesus spoke two millennia ago: "His master replied, 'Well done, good and faithful servant! You have been faithful with a few things; I will put you in charge of many things. Come and share your master's happiness!'" (Matt. 25:21).

At a recent executive retreat, I led my senior staff through an interesting value-sharing exercise to drive home the importance of mentoring our emerging leadership pool. My goal was to have them think of the small group of men and women each is grooming for future leadership. I asked them to imagine that we were shipwrecked on an island with only a radio and eighteen minutes of battery life left, at best. Each of us has two minutes to share with the home office what is most important to remember in case we never make it back. Included in that two-minute communication must be instructions to appoint someone to continue our work should we not return.

This exercise forced two important issues: what we value most and who we trust most to carry on for us. It was a very lively and revealing discussion. Each of us went away renewed in our desire to mentor a select few of our up-and-coming leaders.

BARRIERS TO SUCCESSFUL SUCCESSORS

There are as many unsuccessful leadership transitions as there are successful ones. I imagine that everyone reading this book has witnessed firsthand a leadership transfer that went wrong. The reasons for such fiascos vary but most often include one or more of the following:

➤ The organization doesn't like the new person.

➤ The new person doesn't like the organization.

➤ The new person's family can't adjust to the new city they moved to.

➤ There is a corporate culture conflict: Values and beliefs don't match.

➤ The leader fails miserably in his newly assigned responsibilities: He lacks the ability, capacity, experience, or knowledge to do the job well.

➤ The old guard sabotages the efforts of the new leader.

➤ The old leader sabotages the efforts of the new leader.

➤ The old leader fails to leave, or reappears.

➤ The new leader lacks persistence in implementing changes.

➤ The new leader is recruited away by a better offer or challenge.

➤ The new leader fails to win a following because of poor interpersonal skills.

I have a close friend on the West Coast who has become the general manager of a business his wife's family owns. He worked for his father-in-law for many years before assuming the role of general manager and CEO. The transition has been, and continues to be, a painful one. It seems that family businesses and organizations that are led by founder-CEOs have the worst track record with leadership transitions.

My friend's father-in-law built this successful business with his bare hands—through hardships, the Depression, and decades of sweat and toil. His son-in-law can't seem to do anything right, and dear old Dad never lets him forget it. About a year ago "Dad" and his wife moved to another city to get away from the situation, supposedly to give the son-in-law some room to breathe. But even from that remote site, my friend's father-in-law sows seeds of discord and pessimism through his continued connection to the family and some of the employees in the business. And since Mom- and Dad-in-law are still the major shareholders, their power does not wane.

What is this man's problem? He simply cannot ride off into the sunset, even though he is retired. He cannot let go of something that is so personal to him. To its founders, the family business is a child. You never let go of your emotional attachment to your children. No one can parent the firm the way the founder did, so my poor friend can't win. He continually suffers from high blood pressure that goes up and down directly in proportion to his father-in-law's association with the company. (As a postscript to this story, a decade later my friend left the family business and bought his own company where he is now happy and content. The father-in-law and mother-in-law never changed and died some years later. Their son took over the business and carries on the exact culture of his dad's and the cycle of in-bred dysfunctional family business continues.)

WHY SOME LEADERS CAN'T LET GO

The previous list gives some general reasons why the leadership-succession system can break down and why some leaders in new positions don't last very long. Now let's look at a similar list from a retiring leader's perspective who *needs* to make way for his or her successor. The reasons for not letting go of leadership are powerful ones.

Job security. A retiree may ask himself, *What will I do, and where will I go next? How will I afford to live? Besides, I'm enjoying my work, so why should I think of leaving? Who wants a leader my age? The open slots are being filled by the younger generation.* A leader who is a true servant of the organization will put the group's needs before his or her own.

Fear of retirement. This closely parallels the issue of job security, and

BARRIERS TO GROOMING A SUCCESSOR

- Lack of intrinsic job security or Need for job security
- Insecurity about what to do next
- Fear of retirement
- Resistance to change
- Comfort
- Inflated/Job-associated self-worth or Inferior self-esteem
- The role is your whole life
- Lack of confidence
- Thinking no one else can do the job like you do
- Love for the job
- Loving your leadership role
- Potential loss of further investment in stock, 501(c)(3), 401(k), pension
- Ceasing the human investment and not wanting to let it go

of course, remains for many the ultimate fear—the fear of eventual obsolescence. It is proven that this fear is much greater in men than in women, for men tend to find more of their self-worth from their work.

Resistance to change. We get comfortable with familiar surroundings and routines (a rut is a grave with the ends knocked out) and resist drastic change in our lives. How can I possibly shift to another organization?

It would inconvenience my family to uproot them. It's much easier to stay where I am than to go through the traumatic upheaval of a major geographic and social relocation.

Self-worth. The normal adult (especially male) gains the greatest percentage of his or her identity from his job. To tamper with his job is to interfere with/impinge on his identity. For many leaders, a job is the very essence of his or her self-worth. To lose that role of leadership is to lose confidence and identity. This is especially true of workaholics.

Lack of confidence in a successor. We lack confidence that anyone else will do as good a job as we can do. We can always see reasons to stay another year or season to make sure things get taken care of "properly"— that is, *our* way.

Love for the people and the job. This is perhaps the most emotional reason for hanging on to our jobs. We love our work and we don't want to leave it. Why leave the warmth of our role and organization for the cold realities of a new, alien environment? Why retire to boredom and loneliness when I can hang on with the people I love to be with?

Loss of investment. CEOs, senior pastors, and founders place huge amounts of personal effort into building their organizations. It is an investment that is hard to let go of, much like letting go of children when they leave the nest.

These are all real concerns, yet they do not justify our permanence. Let me speak more candidly about the sixth reason—our love for the people and the job.

THE PAIN OF PARTING

As we tooled down the back roads of what was then East Germany, I couldn't believe we both felt the same way. Somewhere between Dresden and Herrnhut (home of Count Zinzendorf) the tears began to well up in both of our eyes as we awkwardly said our good-byes. We simultaneously realized that it would not be in the future as it had been the last couple of years. We enjoyed being together. Our work in East Germany was going great. Saying good-bye for good was painful, and we wanted to avoid it. Yet it was our choice to go our separate ways.

I had been the country director of our work in East Germany for several years. We had witnessed the joy of seeing a group of East Germans grow in their leadership ability, and now it was time to turn the work over to them. As Werner and I rode down the country roads speaking my native German, my mind flashed years ahead to the day when I would have to send the first of my four children away to college. *I bet it will feel just like this,* I thought. *It's the right thing to do, but oh, so painful to part ways. It will be painful, because it will be permanent. Never again will my children come to live in our home like they did as children, and never again will Werner and I work side-by-side in this ministry in his land.*

Leaving East Germany was the right thing for me to do, but it hurt. Had we not parted, we would still be running the show, and our new leaders would not have geared up to take over. Until we got out of the way, they were content to let us lead, though deep down inside they wanted to take a stab at it themselves. Now we have been gone for years, and they are doing great without us. Does that make me feel insecure? Never! It's all a part of leadership working itself out of a job and moving on to the next. No one is indispensable, and we all have to let go sooner or later.

Our good friend Paul the apostle spent more time training the Christians in the town of Ephesus than with any other group, but he left them eventually. Why? I'm sure they offered him a permanent faculty position and nice housing. He left because there was work for him to do in other places. He trained leaders and then cut them loose with the freedom to build the work in their area. It was a good thing that Paul departed; can you imagine leading in his shadow? Yet, listen to the pain of his departure. We should all wish that the people we lead would feel this way at our retirement parties! "When he had said this, he knelt down with all of them and prayed. They all wept as they embraced him and kissed him. What grieved them most was his statement that they would never see his face again" (Acts 20:36–38).

MENTORING: THE SUCCESSION PROCESS

So how is the process of developing our successors really accomplished? It is a process that has much to do with mentoring. Paul Stanley and Robert Clinton, in their book, *Connecting,* have developed a model of mentoring that they call the "constellation model."

MENTORING CONSTELLATIONS

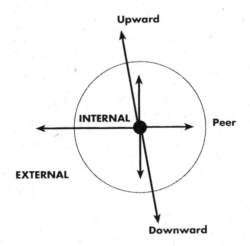

The idea behind the constellation approach to mentoring is that a leader needs all different kinds of mentoring relationships to succeed in his or her leadership. Mentoring includes upward, downward, internal peer, and external peer relationships. I describe them as follows, including my own mentors in each category.

Upward mentoring. First there are leaders who have gone before us, whom we look up to. They hold us accountable and stretch us. We are the leaders who will eventually succeed them. These are the people on my hero wall. Do you remember Arno from chapter 4 on mavericks? Though he has left our organization, he is to this day an important upward mentor. I often look to him to test my ideas. I also love to spend time with two other men who molded my life through the years: Robertson McQuilken, a lifelong personal friend and advisor and former president of Columbia International in Columbia, South Carolina; and Bobby Clinton, my mentor during my doctoral studies at Fuller Seminary in Pasadena, California, in the 1980s.

Downward mentoring. Then there are the people who will one day replace us in our leadership role. They are the small group of people we think about developing into leaders. Some of them are in our own organization; others are outsiders. I first met Andreas in Vienna in 1982. He was a young man right out of graduate school and very confused about his future. We became good friends, and he began to view me as his chief mentor, really as the big brother he never had. More than two decades have gone by, and we are still good friends. And he still looks to me for guidance and advice. He went on to earn a PhD and is today a professor in a prominent university in North Carolina. I am grateful for having had the opportunity to help him find his calling and a fulfilling career.

Internal peer mentoring. Peers within our organization may challenge us to do better. They hold us accountable in our personal lives and in our leadership responsibilities. Receptive leaders can be greatly challenged by others in our group. There are several people in my office who I love spending time with because they never fail to sharpen me. They have gifts in areas where I am weak. I love riding my bike and playing golf with these men to hone my skills—and my character.

External peer mentoring. These are the peer comentoring relationships outside of our organization with people who are roughly at the same stage of maturity and career advancement as we are. The power of networking comes to play in this mentoring process. I have found throughout the years that my best friends are outside of my work environment. I can level with them in a way that I cannot with my coworkers, so this category is more influential for me than with internal mentors. For fifteen years Donna and I have been a part of an annual CEO fellowship retreat. We meet for three days of sharing on many levels. Since we are all leaders of similar organizations, the encouragement factor is huge. I love getting together with these friends whenever possible, for they challenge and probe and stimulate my thinking on the long-range, strategic planning level. When they criticize or question corporate practices and strategies, I listen carefully, for they have nothing at stake except our friendship and the desire to see me do my best. These peers keep me going when I am most discouraged in my own leadership challenges.

I am encouraged by the renewed emphasis on mentoring in the last few years. In Stanley and Clinton's research on leaders who made a difference during their lifetimes, they found that, without exception, these leaders had three to ten people who made significant contributions to each leader's development. In studying major biblical figures and the biographies of great Christian leaders, Stanley and Clinton also concluded that God often used one or more persons to share with and influence those leaders to further develop their leadership abilities.

What makes a good mentor? According to Stanley and Clinton, people who influence the next generation of leaders have these common characteristics:

➤ The ability to readily see potential in a person
➤ Tolerance of mistakes, brashness, abrasiveness, and the like in order to see that potential develop

➤ Flexibility in responding to people

➤ Patience: knowing that time and experience are needed for development

➤ Perspective: having the vision and ability to see down the road and to suggest the next steps a mentee needs to take

➤ Gifts and abilities that build up and encourage others

And how exactly do mentors do their job of mentoring? Again, Stanley and Clinton have identified five important specifics:

➤ Mentors give:

a. Timely advice;

b. Letters, articles, books, or other literature to offer perspective;

c. Finances;

d. Freedom to emerge as a leader even beyond the level of the mentor.

➤ Mentors risk their own reputations in order to sponsor a mentee.

➤ Mentors model various aspects of leadership functions to challenge mentees to move toward them.

➤ Mentors direct mentees to needed resources that will further develop them.

➤ Mentors cominister with mentees in order to increase their confidence, status, and credibility.

FINISHING WELL—FROM MOSES TO TIMOTHY

To end well, we must not get too wrapped up in our own indispensability. Humility is the key to finishing well and passing the torch on to our successors.

One of the keys to a successful leadership transition is to learn to hold our positions loosely. The tighter the grip, the more pride and the harder it becomes to let go at any stage. A loose grip is a humble grip, an attitude that knows our finitude and dispensability. People follow leaders for many reasons. But when that leader's time is done, they quite naturally transfer their loyalty to the next generation.

The Scriptures are filled with good examples of successful leadership transitions based on humility and an understanding of one's own finitude. Following are a few examples.

Moses and Joshua. One of the great examples of a successful leadership transfer is the story of Moses and Joshua in Deuteronomy 34. For forty years Moses looked forward taking his people into the Promised Land. But it was not to be. His successor, Joshua, would be the man to fulfill Moses' dream. In fact, the day before he died Moses was shown the Promised Land and told that his descendants would possess it, but that he would never set foot in it: "I have let you see it with your eyes, but you will not cross over into it" (Deut. 34:4).

How did Moses handle the truth that his successor would have greater success than he, and that Joshua would actually fulfill the objectives Moses himself had sought after for forty years? He handled it with godly grace and dignity: "Now Joshua son of Nun was filled with the spirit of wisdom because Moses had laid his hands on him. So the Israelites listened to him and did what the Lord had commanded Moses" (Deut. 34:9).

The plan worked, the transition was smooth, and the followers immediately transferred their allegiance to Joshua, because his predecessor had in humility placed his hands on Joshua and prayed for God's blessing on his leadership. That is leadership maturity in the final hour, when it probably counts the most.

Jesus and his band of twelve. The entire leadership style of Jesus in his three years of active ministry was to find, select, and train his twelve successors. By the time of the crucifixion, Jesus had only a small band of followers. But he set the pattern for what we call discipleship when he charged them to go and fulfill what he had begun:

"A new command I give you: Love one another. As I have loved you, so you must love one another" (John 13:34).

"Again Jesus said, 'Peace be with you! As the Father has sent me, I am sending you'" (John 20:21).

"Therefore go and make disciples of all nations, baptizing them in the name of the Father and of the Son and of the Holy Spirit, and teaching them to obey everything I have commanded you" (Matt. 28:19–20).

Jesus did not develop Christianity into a worldwide movement, but his early followers did. He chose not to accomplish his will without those who succeeded him. In the same way, our successors will most likely be the ones who finish what we start.

Paul and Timothy. I don't know any place in the New Testament that depicts the development of future leadership more clearly than in 2 Timothy in which Paul charges Timothy, his chief successor, to carry on his work, and to ensure that he in turn finds his own successors: "And the things you have heard me say in the presence of many witnesses entrust to reliable men who will also be qualified to teach others" (2:2).

To survive and grow, a movement such as the Christian faith must go at least four generations: Paul (the first generation) mentored Timothy (second), who was in turn was asked to mentor reliable men (third), who would be qualified to teach others (fourth)—four layers of successors who indeed did spread the infant movement, eventually to every continent. Success without successors is like a childless couple; the future of the family is cut off. In organizational life, a leader who fails to identify and develop his successor stalls the future effectiveness of the organization and hinders the fulfillment of its purposes.

FINAL THOUGHTS

If you're convinced that you need to develop your successors and, in due time, make way for them with humility, here are some ways to tackle any barriers to graceful transition:

Regarding job security. What will you do and where will you go next? A leader who is a true servant of the organization will put the group's needs before his or her own. If it's time to go, then step out by faith and go. Look for another organization that can use your help. I have seen many examples of people who have done this only to find that the leap turned into a great adventure.

Regarding resistance to change. Everyone gets comfortable with familiar surroundings and regular routines. It is only human to resist drastic change. But growth comes from change. There's a woman who has worked in leadership for us in Hong Kong for twenty-five years. She recently decided she needed a change of venue and is looking for a new assignment for her last decade before retirement. I applaud her faith and willingness to leap into this challenge, for she is by nature a very orderly and routine-loving person. The change will not be easy, but she knows it is right and better to try something new.

Regarding fear of retirement. Today we are talking less about retirement and more about prime-time adventures. I refer to "prime time" as that age after traditional retirement. This is a problem as old as work itself. There are many good books and seminars to help people deal with this major life transition. You owe it to yourself and to your organization, as well as to your family, to prepare for retirement. Like airplanes that are decommissioned and taken out of service, a retiree with no plans for useful activity will soon fall apart.

Regarding your self-worth. The normal adult (especially male) gains the greatest portion of his identity from his job. As we have probably seen, this is especially true of workaholics. So what is the answer? Get a life! Find interests outside of work. Find fulfillment and worth in hobbies, sports (doing, not watching), your spouse, children, and community organizations. Get more involved with your church. I've known men and women who eventually found new careers through seeking outside interests. I was recently at a friend's home in San Jose, California. The woman, who is past retirement age, discovered about four years ago that she has a special gift in painting. Now she paints as a new career and sells her work in galleries throughout the Bay Area. How did it happen? A friend dragged her to her first art class four years ago, kicking and screaming!

Regarding a lack of confidence in a successor. Many leaders fall into the trap of having no confidence that anyone else will do as good a job as they can do. There is some justification for such a feeling. Your successor will not start out knowing as much as you know or have as much experience as you have. But don't forget how things were when you were the young upstart. Have faith in the next generation, and come to grips with your own dispensability. The best way to make the transition out of a position of leadership is to make yourself psychologically ready for it long before it happens. Remember, you will do more damage to your organization by staying too long than by leaving too early.

Regarding your love for the people and the job. This is perhaps the most emotional of all the reasons for hanging on. We love our work, and we don't want to leave it. You love your children, yet have to let them leave the nest so they can sprout their own wings of independence. Donna and I have recently entered that empty nest stage as our twins went off to college. It is tough and liberating at the same time. We miss them but love the newfound freedom and adventure for our

next phase of life. In the same way, you owe it to the organization to
let go when the time comes, giving it space to grow without your leadership control. The best defense against depression in this arena is a
good offense: Find something else to replace that which took so much
time in your life. You may be surprised at how much you enjoy the
change.

Regarding your loss of investment. CEOs, senior pastors, and
founders invest huge amounts of emotional, psychological, and personal effort into building their organizations. It is an investment that
is hard to let go of. If you honestly trust the new generation of leadership, then relax and consider your time of leadership as the ground-
work for the successful growth of the organization beyond your direct
involvement. You have not lost an investment, you have made a sub-
stantial contribution in the life of a movement that will succeed in the
future because of your help.

Regarding mentoring constellations. Take some time to reflect on
your mentoring constellations. Read the following questions and make
your own mentoring list:

➤ Who are the people who challenge me to improve
   myself? To whom do I look for stimulation to be my best
   and do my best?

➤ Who are the men or women I am developing to take my
   place when it is my turn to pass the torch? Make that list.

➤ Who are my external peer mentors, who are basically on
   my level and in whom I find great stimulation and
   encouragement? Learn their great value.

➤ Who are my internal peer mentors: those colleagues
   within my own organization through whom I find
   encouragement and stimulation to be and do my best?

Regarding the role of boards of directors. One final word concerning boards of directors: On the issue of successors in leadership, it is imperative that the board takes a strong role in helping present leaders make the transition out as gracefully as possible. In fact, in no area of corporate or church life is there a stronger place to argue for a strong board than in the matter of transition.

A board of directors is charged with the ultimate oversight of the organization. At times a board will have to step in when the older leader is not willing to leave. I can think of two vivid examples of organizations that were at opposite ends of the spectrum in this type of situation. In one case, a weak board had no courage to stand up to the powerful leader who had long outlived his usefulness. The leader stayed and stayed, and it put the organization years behind in its ability to be state-of-the-art in its niche. There was a vacuum of leadership at the helm, and no one was able to fix the problem—from the bottom up or from the top down. By the time that leader did step aside, the organization lost a decade of momentum.

In another case involving a similar type of organization and situation, the board was strong enough to call in consultants, determine that it was time for the founder to move on, and ultimately to ask for his resignation. The process was done with love and firmness. It was painful but effective. A new leader was brought up from the ranks, and that leader has since taken the group to great new heights of ministry. Everyone still appreciates the founder and former CEO, recognizing that he had made his contribution in the founding stages of development.

The board of directors must be the first to transfer loyalty to a new leader and to take a strong role in supporting this new man or woman in his or her new assignment. The people within the organization will follow the lead of the board.

Leadership is a high calling and a great privilege. Those of us who are tapped on the shoulder to lead must do so with an open hand. From our very first day on the job, we need to keep in mind that day in the future when, with humility, we will pass the torch to our successor. How we pass that torch might just be the ultimate measure of our leadership success.

QUICK TIPS FOR LEADERS ON THE GO

Success without Successors
Planning Your Departure the Day You Start

Big Idea: We love to think we are unique and irreplaceable as leaders. But the fact is, we will have to move on some day and leave our legacy to someone else. The last great task of any leader is to work toward a replacement who will pick up where they left off. This task should not be left until the last year of one's tenure, but should be an ongoing process of mentorship with each rising crop of new leaders.

➤ *Pride tightens the grip on leadership, humility relaxes and lets go.* It can be threatening to develop a replacement for many reasons. We can sometimes feel like our worth is tied up in our position. Secure leaders recognize that they are not irreplaceable, and work with humility at cultivating the next generation of leaders.

➤ *Finishing well is an important measure of success in leadership.* Mature leaders are proud of what they have accomplished and have a sense of timing and tenure. There comes a time in the journey when they are ready to turn over leadership to another person. We do not all have the chance to choose our replacements, but we can cultivate a pool of people to pick from who are well qualified.

➤ *Letting go of leadership is like sending your children away to college: It hurts, but has to be done.* There are many reasons why leaders can't let go, but ultimately they have to. The more successful they were, and the longer their tenure, the harder parting will be for them.

➤ *Mentoring is a nonnegotiable function of successful leadership.* There are many ways to get involved with mentoring. Learn how to develop your own mentoring "constellation."

FAILURE TO FOCUS ON THE FUTURE

Prepare Yourself—
It's Later Than You Think

➤ The future is rushing toward us at breakneck speed.

➤ A leader's concentration must not be on the past nor on the present, but on the future.

➤ Vision is an effective leader's chief preoccupation.

➤ Organizations are reinvented with new generations of dreamers.

I f it works, it's obsolete." These words from a futurist sent a chill down my spine. But if leadership is about the future, then the worst thing a leader can do is fear that future. Our present methods are already obsolete, so we constantly refine, improve, listen, and learn. Others may fear, but he or she who leads must boldly face the future.

Consider this letter of caution written in 1829 by future President Martin Van Buren to President Andrew Jackson, cautioning him to put the brakes on the future:

January 31, 1829

To: President Jackson

The canal system of this country is being threatened by the spread of a new form of transportation known as "railroads." The federal government must preserve the canals for the following reasons:

One. If canal boats are supplanted by "railroads," serious unemployment will result. Captains, cooks, drivers, hostlers, repairmen, and lock tenders will be left without means of livelihood, not to mention the numerous farmers now employed in growing hay for horses.

Two. Boat builders would suffer and towline, whip, and harness makers would be left destitute.

Three. Canal boats are absolutely essential to the defense of the United States. In the event of the expected trouble with England, the Erie Canal would be the only means by which we could ever move the supplies so vital to waging modern war.

As you may well know, Mr. President, "railroad" carriages are pulled at the enormous speed of 15 miles per hour by "engines" which, in addition to endangering life and limb of passengers, roar and snort their way through the countryside, setting fire to crops, scaring the livestock, and frightening women and children. The Almighty certainly never intended that people should travel at such breakneck speed.

—Martin Van Buren, Governor of New York (Quoted from "No Growth," *The American Spectator,* Jan. 1984)

In 1829, 15 miles per hour was breakneck speed! As I write this page I am cruising at 37,000 feet above the earth at a speed of 475 miles per hour, comfortably sipping my coffee and typing on a notebook computer. Poor Martin would have a heart attack if he were still with us!

At Yellowstone National Park last summer I saw a vivid illustration of the power of the future. There we were, standing at the crest of the Lower Falls of Yellowstone, the water rushing over the falls millions of gallons at a time, raging and roaring with unbelievable power—a power that mankind tames only with great effort. And I thought, *That water is the future. It comes with such power and nothing can stop it.*

The future is rushing toward us and past us with such awesome power that man can no more stop it than I can stop that raging torrent at Yellowstone.

THE FUTURE IS COMING!

Even though I have passed the benchmark of midlife, my wife, Donna, still accuses me of being a teenager at heart. And of course, part of every teenager's dream is to own a convertible. A couple of years ago, I finally had the chance to scrape up enough money to buy a Mazda Miata. It's nimble, bright red, and loads of fun. I prefer to view it as therapy, not my midlife crisis. I love driving in the mountains here in Colorado with the top down and the breeze blowing through my hair (the little I have left!), forgetting my leadership pressures, concerned only with what fresh scenery the next curve will provide.

I think being a leader is a lot like driving a sports car over a narrow, winding mountain road. As the leader, I am in the driver's seat, holding the steering wheel, and I find myself continually asking these two questions: What's around the next curve? and What is just over the horizon? It could be the greatest opportunity we have ever stumbled upon or a cow in the road that spells disaster! When it comes to the future, whether it's good news or bad news, it's my job to see it coming. In the words of Leroy Eims, "A leader is one who sees more than others see, who sees farther than others see, and who sees before others do" (*Be the Leader You Were Meant to Be*).

To fully exploit this imagery of an organization driving down a road, also think about the past. Some have described the past as a foreign country: *They do things different there.* The world of 1988 was dramatically different from the world of 1968. And the world of 2008 is certainly poles apart from the world of 1988. I believe that our past successes can be our greatest roadblocks to future accomplishments, because what worked in that foreign country of the past will not necessarily work today.

The future is approaching at lightning speed. In 1829 it came at fifteen miles per hour. Today it rushes toward us in quantum leaps. With that future comes changes of earthquake proportions in the way we do whatever we do. Cutting-edge leaders are completely rethinking the nature of organizations and the nature of leadership for the world of tomorrow.

Workers in our organizations are demanding to participate in decisions that are affecting their lives. I sense this more and more as a younger, different kind of workforce fills our ranks. No longer are workers willing to just blindly accept whatever comes down from the top. The democratization of organizations is threatening the very survival of many more traditional organizations. This democratization is forcing us to rethink our very understanding of the role of leaders and leadership and how we structure organizations.

I mentioned these fundamental shifts in our discussions of top-down leadership and dictator decision making in chapters 1 and 5. But they have very much to do with the future as well. We are seeing a continuous trend toward flat organizations. Fewer people believe the centralized institutional approaches have the necessary wisdom or capability to generate progress. Starfish are winning out over the spiders of centralized control. In his landmark book, *The World Is Flat,* Thomas Friedman makes the case that anyone anywhere on earth can compete on a level playing field as long as he or she has a high-speed Internet connection.

The emerging generations, including my own children, have lost confidence in the hierarchical processes of government, church, education, and business. Younger people are just not interested in investing their lives in the maintenance of fostering of our old institutional structures. They want to go where the action is, they want to make a difference, they want to work in new flat organizations, and they want to be in control of their destinies. They are the eBay generation, and would rather work for Google than IBM. The new generations insist on participation in a networking relationship throughout their organization. They prefer a highly decentralized, grassroots approach to problem solving.

THE LEADER'S JOB IS THE FUTURE

"A leader is one who sees more than others see, who sees farther than others see, and who sees before others do."
—Leroy Eims, *Be the Leader You Were Meant to Be*

"Stay one step ahead of your people and you are called a leader. Stay ten steps ahead of your people and you are called a martyr!"
—Source unknown

"Leaders are pioneers. They are people who venture into unexplored territory. They guide us to new and often unfamiliar destinations. People who take the lead are the foot soldiers in the campaigns for change. The unique reason for having leaders—their differentiating function—is to move us forward. Leaders get us going someplace."
—Kouzes and Posner, *The Leadership Challenge*

"Leadership is seeing the consequences of our actions further in the future than those around us can."
—Bill Gothard

One Thing Is Constant: Change

I have had the joy these past fifteen years as the CEO of one organization to work for a wonderful board. The members support me every step of the journey as we have literally changed everything. When they ask me the same question they asked in my first interview, "What is your greatest fear for our organization?" I still come back with the exact same answer. "My greatest fear is irrelevance." I don't want to hand phonograph records to a CD generation or show home movies to a world with YouTube and video iPods.

Change is inevitable; to not change is a sure sign of imminent extinction. Why do you think dinosaurs no longer roam the earth? They could not change as the climate of the earth around them changed. Leaders who don't change with the changing climate of our future world will, like dinosaurs, find themselves only a museum attraction.

> "The most notable trait of great leaders, certainly of great change leaders, however, is their quest for learning. They show an exceptional willingness to push themselves out of their own comfort zones, even after they have achieved a great deal."
> —John Kotter, *Leading Change*

By nature we resist change. Most of us find it hard to see new trends developing in our chosen fields. People are quick to criticize innovations, because the changes frighten them. The effective leader has to help his or her followers feel good about the changes that lie ahead. I have to let my people know that they can trust me to take care of them—that I won't lead them to a dead end.

Once people said that cars would never replace the horse and carriage. Others said that the light bulb wasn't really better than the kerosene lamp. Then there were the naysayers who said that movies could never entertain like vaudeville could. On the heels of those negative attitudes came the condemnation of television, which people were sure would never supplant radio as the primary source of entertainment. The entertainment industry fought the VHS and DVD inventions, because they thought it would put theaters out of business!

When Alexander Graham Bell invented the telephone, people laughed him out of town. Certainly people were not ready for such an instrument, whereby people could talk to one another through a wire over great distances! Leaders have to lead into the future despite the naysayers and opposition.

DREAMERS AND VISIONS

One of my first jobs as a teenager was as a busboy at a local Big Boy restaurant in my hometown of Huntsville, Alabama. Why did I work at that restaurant? One reason was to make money. And of course, I got paid by the hour.

Today I don't get paid by the hour, I get paid for results. And I don't work today for the purpose of a paycheck. I like to think that my main drive is to make a difference and to have an impact on the future of my

VISION

"To choose a direction, a leader must first have developed a mental image of a possible and desirable future state of the organization. This image, which we call a vision, may be as vague as a dream or as precise as a goal or mission statement. The critical point is that a vision articulates a view of a realistic, credible, attractive future for the organization, a condition that is better in some important ways than what now exists."
—Warren Bennis and Burt Nanus, *Leaders*

"Vision for ministry is a clear mental image of a preferable future imparted by God to His chosen servants and is based upon an accurate understanding of God, self, and circumstances."
—George Barna, *The Power of Vision*

"There is no more powerful engine driving an organization toward excellence and long-range success than an attractive, worthwhile, achievable vision for the future, widely shared."
—Burt Nanus, *Visionary Leadership*

organization. I get paid to lead us into the future. I couldn't have cared less about the future of that Big Boy restaurant back in the 1960s.

Leaders are paid to be a dreamers. In fact, the higher you go in leadership, the more your work is about the future. I have very little influence on what is going to happen in my organization in the next six months, but I am making daily decisions that could have a profound impact on us five years down the road.

Some may ask in frustration, "How can I drain the swamp? How can I plan for the future when I'm up to my neck in alligators?" The tyranny of the urgent always fights against our planning and thinking time, but if we don't make the time to plan for the future, we will be its victims. We will develop a style of reactionary leadership. What is needed is proactive leadership that anticipates the future. Proactive leaders are the ones who have the most profound impact on the world. One such visionary leader was Walt Disney. Has anyone in North America not been influenced by this dreamer? Listen to his portrayal of the future, before the ground was broken for Disneyland in Anaheim:

> The idea of Disneyland is a simple one. It will be a place for people to find happiness and knowledge. It will be a place for parents and children to spend pleasant times in one another's company. A place for teachers and pupils to discover great ways of understanding and education. Here the older generation can recapture the nostalgia of days gone by, and the younger generation can savor the challenge of the future. Here will be the wonders of nature and man for all to see and understand. Disneyland will be based upon and dedicated to the ideals, the dreams, and hard facts that have created America. And it will be uniquely equipped to dramatize these dreams and facts and send them forth as a source of courage and inspiration to all the world.

Disneyland will be something of a fair, an exhibition, a playground, a community center, a museum of living facts, and a showplace of beauty and magic. It will be filled with the accomplishments, the joys and hopes of the world we live in. And it will remind us and show us how to make those wonders part of our lives. (B. Thomas, *Walt Disney: An American Original*, 246)

Leadership must devote itself to goals and strategies. Leaders ask, "Where are we going next, and why are we going there?" Managers ask, "How will we get there?" We need organizations today that have this balanced dose of visionary leadership and effective management. "We are more in need of a vision or destination and a compass (a set of principles or directions) and less in need of a road map," says Stephen Covey in *The Seven Habits of Highly Effective People*. Covey clarifies the difference in management and leadership when he says, "management is efficiency in climbing the ladder of success; leadership determines whether the ladder is leaning against the right wall" (101).

DREAMERS

"All men dream; but not equally. Those who dream by night in the dusty recesses of their minds Awake to find that it was vanity; But the dreamers of day are dangerous men, That they may act their dreams with open eyes to make it possible."
—T. E. Lawrence, quoted in Bennis and Nanus, *Leaders*

BECOMING A LEARNING ORGANIZATION

While I was jogging recently in a town away from our home, I could not help but stop in front of a house that had a square marble stone in its front yard. It caught my eye as unusual—a stone marker in a front yard?

The house looked a bit eccentric, not your run-of-the-mill suburban home. On the marker were these words: "On This Spot in 1897, Nothing Happened." I ran off feeling foolish for being taken for a ride. It would not surprise me if someone were watching from a window to see how I reacted!

As I jogged on, the truth of that marker hit me. My greatest fear for the future of the organization I lead is that it would be said, "after our first 50 years ... nothing happened."

Whether we like it or not, we are in the midst of a paradigm revolution. Things are changing dramatically on the economic, technological, sociological, generational, and spiritual fronts. If we don't flex in response to external changes, we will become obsolete. The great opportunities of tomorrow will be seized by the younger, more aggressive groups who do respond. They may not do things the way we think they ought to be done, but the reality is that they will be used despite themselves to get things done.

> "My interest is in the future because I am going to spend the rest of my life there."
> —Charles F. Kettering

Futurist Alvin Toffler said, "The illiterate of the twenty-first century will not be those who cannot read or write, but those who cannot learn, unlearn, and relearn." Peter Senge, in *The Fifth Discipline*, wrote, "The ability to learn faster than your competitors may be the only sustainable competitive advantage." There are two ways to approach the future: as learners or as closed experts. The opposite of the learner is the know-it-all, whose type of management has the attitude that they have mastered their trade. With rock-solid policies and procedures built on years of experiences and tradition, why should they change? The old way is not only the best way, but really the only way.

This is what I call the "pro attitude": "We're the pros at this; others can look to us and see how it ought to be done." Christian organizations have the added paralysis of hiding behind their spiritual views—theologizing their methodology. The years of organizational tradition become a sacred cow that cannot and should not be tampered with. After all, it was created by our spiritual forefathers, who were led by God to create the organization we now inherit.

A vivid current example comes from the world of photography. Kodak dominated the world of cameras and film for generations, until the surprise popularity of the digital camera. They knew about the new technology, but chose to ignore it. It was their estimate that digital cameras would be slow to catch on, and they missed the paradigm shift by five years. As they were asleep at the wheel of traditional film, the Japanese muscled in on the market and the world went digital early and fast at the surprise of Kodak. By the time Kodak made the shift, it was too late for many workers. Forty thousand employees lost their jobs in Rochester, New York, as a result of the missed shift to a new technology. The world changed, Kodak did not, and the rest is history. As with the world of time-keeping, the Japanese now dominate the world of digital cameras as well.

In *Changing the Essence,* Richard Beckhard and Wendy Pritchard speak of this issue that plagues all older traditional organizations: "The assumptions that guided organizations in the past were that they could control their own destinies and that they operated in a relatively stable and predictable environment" (2).

Beckhard and Pritchard call the changes in the external environments in which we must work "whitewater" turbulence: explosion of technology, changes in the political landscape, new relationships between the First and Third Worlds, worldwide changes in social values, the role of women, and the changing balance of financial wealth in the world (1).

In our own organization I see the desperate need for change. Just because we have had some success in the past is no guarantee that the future is bright. I am not saying that there's anything deadly wrong with us. The problem is that the world outside is changing; the international community we want to touch is changing; our new workforce is different, with different expectations; and our donor base is changing dramatically. All across the United States, churches are thinking differently about financial priorities. And the peoples in the nations we serve are thinking differently about our relationships to them.

FAITH AND THE FUTURE

The future is coming. "When all else is lost, the future still remains," remarked Christian Nestell Bovee. The Bible has a lot to say about the future; in fact, it is a book for futurists. Whole books of the Bible are devoted to the future in the form of divine prophecies—books like Daniel, Isaiah, and many of the minor prophets. In the New Testament, the book of Revelation is devoted to an unfolding of what the future will hold as the Creator wraps up history as we know it.

I have read many books about the future, written by futurists. I enjoy them, but I read them with skepticism. Futurists do have the ability to predict trends based on solid scientific analysis, but they cannot know the future any more than astrologers can know it. The Bible is clear that no man or woman on earth knows the future: "Since no man knows the future, who can tell him what is to come?" (Eccl. 8:7).

If you are the kind of person who tends to fear the future, then find comfort in the promises of God for his people. The Bible is very encouraging about the long-term future: "Let this be written for a future generation, that a people not yet created may praise the Lord" (Ps. 102:18).

"For I know the plans I have for you," declares the Lord, "plans to prosper you and not to harm you, plans to give you hope and a future" (Jer. 29:11).

FINAL THOUGHTS

Creating vision and direction for the future is one of the primary responsibilities of leadership. The leader must plan for the future. He or she must direct or head the team in developing organizational goals, plans, and strategies that flow out of a crisp purpose or vision statement.

Notice I include "the team" in this. As we have seen, people throughout the organization are shareholders in the group and want a part in planning for the future. The leaders who surround the top person should play an integral part in shaping vision and making plans. When the team has a stake in goal formation, they have a vested interest in goal ownership and in seeing these goals fulfilled.

Here is some concrete advice about building for the future:

Set aside time to think about the future. I call this institutional navel gazing. It may not be all that fun, but we have to take time to study ourselves up close and personal. At least quarterly, I get away just to contemplate the future, from one to ten years out. It is important to take time away from the swamp and forget about the alligators nipping at your neck! I find that my best time for future thinking is out of the office, in fact, that is a requirement for me. Keep a Future file in your computer, where you can store your dreams away from the prying eyes of the bureaucrats and pragmatists. Above all, take time to dream. My dream file is a

> "In times of change,
> learners inherit the earth,
> while the learned find
> themselves
> beautifully equipped,
> to deal with a world
> that no longer exists."
> —Robin Cook, *Abduction*

Word document on my laptop where I keep my dreams, goals, and wild ideas about the future. It is also filled with inspirational quotes that I glean along the way.

The first step in the right direction is a healthy understanding of your present position. Take the time to ask insiders and outsiders how they feel about the strengths and weaknesses of your organization. Perform a vision audit in which you send out questionnaires and ask for honest feedback. Then gather the respondents together in small focus groups to discuss their feedback. Learning organizations are not afraid to hear the truth. Six of the most important questions to ask are:

1. What are the strengths of our group?
2. What are our weaknesses?
3. What should our highest priorities be?
4. What do we do well?
5. What do we do poorly?
6. What barriers do we need to remove to fundamentally enhance our effectiveness for the future?

Develop a fresh vision statement. Even if your organization is fifty or a hundred years old, new times require fresh expressions of the group's passion. Some call them purpose statements, but I prefer the term *vision,* because it seems fresher and more animated. Burt Nanus, in *Visionary Leadership,* defines vision as simply "a realistic, credible, attractive future for your organization. Selecting and articulating the right vision, this powerful idea is the toughest task and the truest test of great leadership" (16, 28–29).

He goes on to state that powerful and transforming visions always tend to have the following special properties:

➤ They are appropriate for the organization and the time.
➤ They set standards of excellence and reflect high ideals.

➤ They clarify purpose and direction.

➤ They inspire enthusiasm and encourage commitment.

➤ They are well articulated and easily understood.

➤ They reflect the uniqueness of the organization.

➤ They are ambitious.

Get together and set strategic goals. It is important to have a set of flexible, changing long- and short-term goals. I work with my direct reports to create an annual theme and set the goals we hope to accomplish in that year. I ask them to give me three to five top goals they hope to accomplish outside of the norm of their regular responsibilities.

One piece of simple advice on goal setting: When you list a set of goals for your mission, they should be SMART goals:

➤ Specific

➤ Measurable

➤ Attainable

➤ Relevant

➤ Trackable

> "Concentration is the key to economic results. No other principle of effectiveness is violated as constantly today as the basic principle of concentration.... Our motto seems to be, 'Let's do a little bit of everything.'"
> —Peter Drucker, *Classic Drucker: Wisdom from Peter Drucker, from the Pages of Harvard Business Review*

Concentrate and eliminate. Lyle Schaller observes that most churches are ineffective, not because they do too little but because they attempt too much. The German poet Johann Wolfgang von Goethe put it this way: The key to life is concentration and elimination. Leadership must give itself to articulating a clear purpose statement and a set of corporate goals that the company can buy into. Then the organization can focus and concentrate its resources on doing specifically what it is there to do, instead of dissipating energies by dabbling in a little bit of everything.

Not a week goes by when I am not confronted with another great opportunity that our organization should jump on board with. After my initial excitement, I sit back and ask myself, *How does this square with what God has called us to do in the world?* If it is not going to lead to the fulfillment of our basic goals, we should not get involved.

Read all about it. Take time to read books about future trends by experts in your field. A number of writers spend their energy studying trends that affect all of us no matter what our endeavor. Go through my list of references at the end of this book and choose to read some of those great books. Go to the library or a bookstore and peruse the magazine rack and some of the creative publications that could help you. Here are my favorite magazines for breeding new ideas about the future:

➤ *Fast Company*

➤ *INC*

➤ *WIRED*

➤ *Entrepreneur*

Attempt and expect great things. I am an eternal optimist. I know who holds the future, and I know that I am eternally secure in his hands of control. Sure, bad things happen to good people, but ultimately history will unfold exactly as God has planned from the beginning. My passion is to

LEADERSHIP VISIONS ARE SNAPSHOTS OF THE FUTURE

"A vision is a picture of a future state for the organization, a description of what it would like to be a number of years from now. It is a dynamic picture of the organization in the future, as seen by its leadership. It is more than a dream or set of hopes, because top management is demonstrably committed to its realization: it is a commitment."
—Richard Beckhard and Wendy Pritchard, *Changing the Essence*

"I am a dreamer. Some men see things as they are, and ask why; I dream of things that never were, and ask why not?"
—George Bernard Shaw

be all that I can be in the full potential he has given me and that I do all that he wants me to do in my short walk on this planet (see Phil. 3:12). For the organizations that I help lead, I expect of them no less than I expect from myself: Anticipate the future aggressively in the spirit of William Carey, who declared to his critics as he left for India 200 years ago to be a positive force in a needy place, "Expect great things, attempt great things."

QUICK TIPS FOR LEADERS ON THE GO

FAILURE TO FOCUS ON THE FUTURE

Prepare Yourself—It's Later Than You Think

Big Idea: Leaders get paid to think about the future. It is the job of a leader to anticipate the opportunities and threats that await an organization around the next curve. Such thoughts should be crafted into a vision statement to help propel the organization in the right direction. To ignore the future is to fail as a leader.

> ➤ *The future is rushing at us at breakneck speed.* The pace of change intensifies with every year. It seems like the shelf life of useful ideas gets shorter every month. Today's leaders must study the future as they become "futurists" in their particular discipline.

> ➤ *A leader's concentration must not be on the past nor on the present, but on the future.* The past is finished. Whatever happened there cannot be undone. The present is being dealt with on the basis of yesterday's plans. That leaves only the future as the focus of an effective leader. To neglect the future is the biggest mistake a leader can make.

> ➤ *Vision is an effective leader's chief preoccupation.* Above mentoring, communicating, and paying attention to

people, a leader must obsess about the future. Vision is essential to every effective leader.

➤ *Organizations are reinvented with new generations of dreamers.* Dreamers, from Walt Disney to Dr. Martin Luther King Jr. to Billy Graham to Mother Teresa, changed the world by envisioning a state of things better than before. Businesses and churches need these kinds of dreamers to stay relevant in a changing world. Recruit dreamers. Spend time as leaders dreaming about what could be.

AFTERWORD

I originally wrote *The Top Ten Mistakes Leaders Make* in the early 1990s. I had just turned forty and was relatively young in my leadership experience as a new CEO. The success of this book over the years has been encouraging, especially since most books by unknown authors never go into a second printing. I have heard from so many readers who could empathize with the issues I brought up. Most of the people I hear from suffer in some way under leaders who still don't get it: the servant collaborative leadership style. They write to say thank you for giving them hope and new ideas of how to do leadership right. With all that has been written about empowering leadership styles, my observation still holds true that it is not a natural part of human nature. Unless leaders are out there learning and opening themselves to different ideas on how to lead, most will continue to default toward top-down leadership.

Fifteen years have passed since those far away days of the early nineties. The past is a foreign country now, and we live in a very different leadership culture. Many people ask me the question, "Are your top ten principles still the same? Are they still relevant? Would you now focus on a different list of ten?" Honestly, I pondered this very question a lot as I worked on this updated version of the book, and I still come up with the same top ten mistakes leaders make. But I assure you, in recent years I have come up with another twenty or so that could easily be formed into another couple of books!

The other point I wish to make regarding the time that has elapsed since I first published this book in the early nineties is the fact that an entirely new generation of young leaders is emerging. Some of the characteristics of these up-and-coming leaders are described in chapters one and nine. Let me tell you—I am excited about these new leaders in their twenties and thirties, and for my part I hope I can mentor them along in their journey. It is my desire to see them take servant leadership to a whole new level, and not repeat the mistakes of older generations. So listen up, and learn to let them lead.

—Hans Finzel

Highlands Ranch, Colorado

REFERENCES

Autry, James A. 1991. *Love and Profit*. New York: William Morrow. Used with permission.

Barker, Joel. 1992. *Future Edge*. New York: William Morrow. Used with permission.

Barna, George. 1992. *The Power of Vision*. Ventura, CA: Regal.

Beckhard, Richard, and Wendy Pritchard. 1992. *Changing the Essence*. San Francisco: JosseyBass. Used with permission.

Bennis, Warren. 1989. *On Becoming a Leader*. New York: AddisonWesley.

Bennis, Warren, and Burt Nanus. 1985. *Leaders: The Strategies for Taking Charge*. New York: HarperCollins. Used with permission.

Blanchard, Ken. 2004. *The Heart of a Leader*. Colorado Springs: David C. Cook.

Bradford, Lawrence J., and Claire Raines. 1992. *Twenty something*. New York: Master Media. Used with permission.

Brafman, Ori, and Rod Beckstrom. 2006. *The Starfish and the Spider: The Unstoppable Power of Leaderless Organizations*. New York: Portfolio.

Cook, Robin. 2000. *Abduction*. New York: Berkley.

Collins, Jim, and Jerry Porras. 2004. *Built to Last*. New York: HarperCollins.

Ibid. 2001. *Good to Great*. New York: Random.

Covey, Stephen. 1991. *The Seven Habits of Highly Effective People*. New York: Simon & Schuster.

DePree, Max. 1987. *Leadership Is an Art*. New York: Doubleday. Used with permission.

Drucker, Peter. 1990. *Managing the Nonprofit Organization*. New York: HarperCollins.

Ibid. 1994. *Post-Capitalist Society*. New York: HarperCollins.

Eims, Leroy. 1975. *Be the Leader You Were Meant to Be*. Wheaton, IL: Victor.

Erwin, Gayle. 1988. *The Jesus Style*. Waco, TX: Word.

Greenleaf, Robert K. 1977. *Servant Leadership*. New York: Paulist.

Hersey, Paul, and Ken Blanchard. 1982. *Management of Organizational Behavior: Utilizing Human Resources*. Englewood Cliffs, NJ: Prentice Hall. Used with permission.

Killman, Ralph. 1984. *Beyond the Quick Fix*. San Francisco: JosseyBass.

Kotter, John. 1996. *Leading Change*. Boston: Harvard.

Ibid. 1999. *What Leaders Really Do*. Boston: Harvard.

Kouzes, James, and Barry Posner. 1988. *The Leadership Challenge*. San Francisco: JosseyBass. Used with permission.

Lencioni, Patrick. 2000. *The Four Obsessions of an Extraordinary Executive*. San Francisco: JosseyBass.

Maxwell, John. 1993. *Developing the Leader within You*. Nashville: Thomas Nelson. Used with permission of John Maxwell and INJOY.

McGregor, Douglas. 1985. *The Human Side of Enterprise*. New York: McGraw Hill.

Nanus, Burt. 1992. *Visionary Leadership*. San Francisco: JosseyBass.

Nouwen, Henri J. 1974. *Out of Solitude*. Notre Dame: Ave Maria.

Peters, Tom. 1991. "Management Excellence," *The Business Journal. Chicago Tribune*. September 9, 1991.

Ibid. 1992. *Liberation Management*. New York: Alfred Knopf.

Peters, Tom, and Robert Waterman. 1982. *In Search of Excellence*. New York: Warner.

Reeves, R. Daniel. 1993. "Societal Shifts," *Ministry Advantage*. May/June 1993. Pasadena, CA: Charles E. Fuller.

Rodgers, Buck, and Irving M. Levey. 1987. *Getting the Best out of Yourself and Others*. New York: HarperCollins. Used with permission.

Sanders, J. Oswald. 1967. *Spiritual Leadership*. Chicago: Moody.

Sanny, Lorne. 1992. "Leadership," *The Business Ministry Journal*. July/August 1992.

Shaw, George Bernard. 1972. *Man and Superman*. Baltimore: Penguin.

Stanley, Paul, and J. Robert Clinton. 1992. *Connecting*. Colorado Springs: NavPress. Used with permission.

Thomas, B. 1976. *Walt Disney: An American Tradition*. New York: Simon & Schuster.

Tichy, Noel, and Stratford Sherman. 1993. *Control Your Destiny or Someone Else Will*. New York: Currency Doubleday.

Van Buren, Martin. 1984. "No Growth," *America Spectator*. January 1984.